T0269749

corker

corker

A DEEPLY UNSERIOUS WINE BOOK

HANNAH
CROSBIE

EBURY
PRESS

1

Ebury press, an imprint of Ebury Publishing
20 Vauxhall Bridge Road
London SW1V 2SA

Ebury Press is part of the Penguin Random House group of companies whose
addresses can be found at global.penguinrandomhouse.com

First published by Ebury Press in 2024

www.penguin.co.uk

A CIP catalogue record for this book is available from the British Library

ISBN 9781529913163

Design: Claire Rochford

Typeset in 10/13 pt Baskerville Pro by Jouve (UK), Milton Keynes
Printed and bound in Great Britain by Clays Ltd, Elcograf S.p.A.

The authorised representative in the EEA is Penguin Random House Ireland,
Morrison Chambers, 32 Nassau Street, Dublin D02 YH68

Penguin Random House is committed to a sustainable future
for our business, our readers and our planet. This book is made from
Forest Stewardship Council® certified paper.

For my English teachers, who probably now wish they hadn't told me I could write.

CONTENTS

INTRODUCTION

'I must have some booze. I demand to have some booze!'
RICHARD E GRANT, WITHNAIL AND I

—

I love wine. I love everything about it. I love pouring it, swirling it and holding it up to the light to watch it glow. I love thumbing through atlases and wine journals to acquire the right words for it, and then working these words into tasting notes. I love writing about it. I love scrubbing it out of white cotton shirts, off my purple teeth, off other people's sofas. I love how port is the colour of a recently acquired bruise and how the smell of Beaujolais reminds me of a friend. I love green bottles that wrap around restaurant walls. I love how, when opened at the right time, wine can catalyse the most important conversations in our lives, how it can leave us inspired from a lunch, or propel us into a promising nighttime. I love damp cellars that remind me of my grandfather's workroom. I love catching a glimpse of a vintage at its peak, but I relish the melancholy that comes with tipping a dying bottle down the drain. I love learning about pruning methods, I love ordering for the table, I love watching a truly gifted sommelier at work. I love everything about wine, but let's get one thing straight before you read another sentence: this is not a serious wine book. Allow me to explain.

I'm fortunate enough to spend my life disguising an obsession as a career. I make a living talking about wine online and on TV, with the intention of getting more people as fascinated with it as I am. There's an overwhelming amount of information out there, but I wilfully believe that there's no such thing as a stupid question. Naturally, this opens me up to an avalanche of curious drinkers looking for advice. A lot of these messages are people asking me for wine recommendations.

Through this, a new way of drinking wine has become searingly apparent. Nowadays, very rarely do I get asked, 'Hannah, I'm having a fillet of salmon tonight, what should I drink with it?' Seemingly, fewer of you want to know what to pair with specific dishes, which comes as no surprise. You know exactly where to go for that sort of thing. There is a wealth of information out there, not only on the internet, but in many brilliantly written books that have a solution for every gastronomic query: from jam doughnuts to jamon beurre (my favourites are Victoria Moore's *Wine Dine Dictionary* and *Which Wine When* by Bert Blaize and Claire Strickett). Plus, most of the younger wine drinkers I speak to have resigned themselves to the fact they may never own a house, so are choosing to engage in an inspiring culinary nihilism, spending a great deal of their extra income on eating out, where a skilled sommelier will pair wine with their food far better then they ever could at their (rented) home.

Instead, I've found that a lot of you are approaching wine in a different way. Rather than foods, it's *situations* that I'm asked to pair wines with. Perhaps you're meeting your girlfriend's parents for the first time, and you want to bring a bottle that will somehow convey to her parents that you have a bed frame. Perhaps you just quit your job and want something to celebrate. Perhaps you've just been dumped. Perhaps you're doing the dumping. Or perhaps you're going to a barbecue. The drinking habits of this new generation are informed by a new set of criteria: rapidly expanding tastes, a keenness to experiment and, most pressingly, ever-climbing living costs.

Wine has seeped into every corner of our lives. It punctuates every mouthful and remark with a sip, lubricating conversation like a good joke. The wine list of my favourite restaurant has nearly doubled in size over the past year. No pub, deli, airport lounge or train journey is safe from at least a can of wine concealed in a breast pocket. But if wine is ubiquitous, why does the stuff still feel so unfamiliar? Why do we look at our wine lists with the type of bewildered panic usually reserved for unopened letters from HMRC or the first time we see a parent smoke a cigarette?

This book is here to help. Alongside a number of different social, and antisocial situations that necessitate a bottle, I've given my suggestions for which wines could be a worthy match. Some of these are rooted in practicality and extensive supermarket/wine bar/train station/breastfeeding/inflight menu research. Some are deeply unserious, purely anecdotal explorations of the joy of everyday drinking. If you're looking for wine writing that takes itself seriously, look somewhere else. Literally, anywhere else.

There are, of course, a multitude of remarkable wines to drink at a picnic or on a holiday that I haven't suggested. So, it's worth noting that this book is in no way exhaustive or prescriptive, it's a starting point to get you to think about exactly what kind of wines you like and in which situations you might drink them. It pays attention to things such as taste, terroir and history, as well as often overlooked things like cost, availability and whether you can get a bottle from the big Sainsbury's near your parents' house in Buttfuck Nowhere at Christmastime. The things that normal people care about.

But why should you take my word for it?

I made the switch from waiter and wine pourer to professional wine writer a little over five years ago and, thanks to you, reading this book, my life has been completely transformed. I've tasted thousands of wines and written hundreds of thousands of words about the ones I prize. I've met, worked with and been influenced by a brilliant, passionate cohort of sommeliers, buyers, writers, communicators and winemakers. I've indulged in many sore-sided Pinot-stained, teary-eyed evenings with the ones I have the estimable privilege to know personally. But I've found that a lot of the wine world takes itself very, very seriously indeed. There is a side of the industry that is, for lack of a better phrase, comedically challenged.

I believe that this seriousness is one of the main reasons people lack confidence when it comes to wine. They think that, although wine is not their career, they ought to possess that same knowledge and seriousness before even attempting an interest in wine. I take my winged eyeliner and my tax returns very seriously, everything else is inconsequential. Do I love wine? Yes. Do I devote my every waking moment to hunting down the best bottles I can, drinking them and writing about them? With pleasure. Is it the single most important entity in my life? Would I die for it? Fuck, no. We have families and a climate crisis to prioritise. Wine remains one of the biggest loves of my life. But at the end of the day, as many of my peers remind me when I'm obsessing over pronouncing Xarel·lo wrong, it's all just fermented grape juice. The world of wine really isn't as intimidating as it first may feel, you just need to find voices and opinions you trust. Despite this, it persists as a stress for many people, whether they just took their first sip of Pinot Grigio or they've been casually drinking it for decades.

The fear of people laughing at you for getting it wrong is mostly an irrational one, but there are, sadly, still circles where wine pedants *will* point the finger when you enjoy something a bit differently ('You put *ice* in your rosé?') or make an easy mistake ('Erm, it's Pouilly-Fuissé, not Pouilly-*Fumé* . . .').

This frustrates me enormously. The paralysing anxiety about whether we're doing wine 'right' can mean we overlook its primary purpose. Pleasure. Celebration. Whatever happened to getting drunk with friends? Most wine is not drunk in the tasting room, it is drunk on our sofas, it is shared while sitting on our friends' sideboards, slurped from a tin in the passenger seats of their cars. I think, because of this, the average drinker thinks of these experiences as unimportant, which is a great shame. When wine seems to divide people rather than bring them together, I can't help but feel we're getting it a little bit wrong. Why choose between searching for value and building your knowledge? You can get drunk on cheap wine and still be endlessly curious about the complex, ever-changing environment that contextualises it. You

should be able to do both. You should be able to have your Claret and *drink* it.

That is why *Corker* exists, to bridge the world of wine into ordinary experiences, pulling it out of private dining rooms and echoing cellars and into our domestic lives. Because of this, this book might feel a different to others you've read that delve deep into wines' intricacies. It simplifies; it focuses on real situations lived by normal people. It states without apology that you can enjoy a vast range of wine without having an encyclopaedic knowledge of it. Come on in, the water's fine. And if I manage to pull in a few of you in with me, then as far as I'm concerned, this book has done its job.

GLOSSARY

Life's too short to be reading a glossary. It'll be even shorter if you plan on drinking everything in this book. So, for the sake of both ease and sanity, I've made this glossary and short and painless as possible. You need only consult this guide when you stumble across something you're unfamiliar with. I've split the glossary into two sections: words about wine and words about winemaking. Easy.

WORDS ABOUT WINE

ABV: Stands for 'Alcohol by Volume'. This is the unit used to measure alcoholic strength in wine and is recorded as a percentage. You can usually find it on the back of a wine bottle. Read more on alcohol and its effect on a wine below.

ACIDITY: When people say they like 'dry' wine (see overleaf), I think they sometimes confuse it with a wine that's acidic. Acidity is what makes your mouth water, and a good wine will have an acidity in balance with the rest of the wine. Wines also need a high acidity to be able to age effectively.

ALCOHOL: Obviously a wine will have alcohol, Hannah, why have you included this in the glossary? Well, as true as this may be, not all wines have the same level of alcohol. And it's good to be armed with information about what's normal for wine, so you don't leave a situation more drunk than you ought to be. Your toilet bowl will thank you for it. For reference: low-alcohol wines are below 11%, high-alcohol wines are above 14%, and wines with medium alcohol are everything in between.

APPELLATION: You'll see this word on wine bottles and hear it in conversation. An appellation is a legally defined and protected geographical area in France. Other winemaking countries have their own classification systems, where in order to put a specific appellation or winemaking area on a bottle, the wine needs to meet a certain set of criteria. For example, the wine may only be made from a list of certain grapes, or the wine may need to be aged for a minimum amount of time before it is released. All of these rules and regulations can be pretty painstaking to achieve, so seeing a named appellation or winemaking area on a label means you can be pretty confident on the style and quality of the wine in the bottle.

CRU: This term originated from France, but you'll hear it broadly used when referring to a vineyard (or vineyards) of superior quality. To maintain this quality, grand or premier cru wines are subject to rigorous rules and regulations (see appellation above) to be able to name the cru on the label. Oh, and grand cru is a step above premier cru. You still with me? Good.

CUVÉE: This is a French term used in a multitude of scenarios, but the most common one (and the only example I'll use in this book) is to describe a particular wine from a producer. For example: 'Which was your favourite cuvée we tasted from that producer?'

DRY: When I worked in restaurants and would ask a table what kind of wine they'd like, every night I'd be told, 'A dry wine, please.' It seems that the word 'dry' is one of the only technical wine terms used in common parlance, but beware. Strictly speaking, nearly all wine is 'dry', meaning you can't taste any residual sugar on the palate. Cabernet Sauvignon is dry, Pinot Grigio is dry, Chardonnay is dry. I know. The world is a crazy place.

NEW WORLD / OLD WORLD: The concept of New and Old World is becoming a little outdated, but you'll still hear this when people talk about winemaking countries. Old World winemaking countries tend to refer those in Western Europe, with centuries-old winemaking traditions; places like France, Italy and Spain. Countries that are patronisingly referred to as 'New World' include South Africa, America and New Zealand, even though they have fruitful and and diverse winemaking cultures of their own, many of which are several centuries old.

OAKED: When we wine people refer to a wine as oaked, this means that it's obvious that it has spent some time ageing in barrels. During this time, notes (known as secondary notes) are imparted into the wine, but exactly how much depends on how much the staves (the single slats of wood that make up the barrel) are toasted by fire when they are bent and shaped into barrels. Lightly toasted staves bring an aroma of sweet vanilla, whereas those that are heavily toasted suggest espresso and coconut. Some winemakers would rather add oak chips into the wine to artificially give the wine heavily oaked notes. Some people like this. Some people are weirdos.

PÉT-NAT (PÉTILLANT-NATUREL): Love it or loathe it, wines made in the pétillant-naturel style (meaning naturally sparkling) have been around for a long time, and certainly aren't going anywhere. Made popular recently by the natural wine craze, these are lightly sparkling wines that only go through one fermentation, kickstarted by the yeasts already naturally present on the grape, and are sealed with a crown cap.

TANNINS: You'll hear this word a lot when chatting to sommelier-types, particularly when referring to red wine. Tannins are a type of chemical compound extracted from the seeds, skins and pips of grapes. I usually describe it as that stemmy, rough mouthfeel you get when you have the last dregs of a leftover cup of green tea. This sounds totally vile on its own, but as part of a harmonious mouthfeel, tannins contribute to the body and balance of a wine. Plus, they bind to proteins and help break them down, hence why particularly tannic red wines are a good match for tough meat.

TERROIR: There are many definitions of the term 'terroir', but the one that resonates with me the most is 'a sense of place'. Terroir is not measurable, or legally defined, it's an intangible way of describing the results of a region's climate, geographical makeup and location. A true expression of an appellation's terroir means that a well-made wine tastes as if it could only come from that specific place.

VARIETAL WINE: An opposite of a blend, this is a wine made wholly from one type of grape. For example, 100% Chardonnay or 100% Merlot.

VARIETY: You'll hear this word used interchangeably with 'grape'. For example, Pinot Noir, Sauvignon Blanc and Pinot Grigio are all grape varieties. There are around 4,000 of them in the world but, mercifully, you'll only be introduced to the most common in this book.

VINTAGE: This is another way of referring to the year in which the grapes were harvested to make a wine, hence why you'll hear the phrases 'a good vintage' and 'a good year' used pretty interchangeably. Non-vintage wine is wine made from a blend of vintages, usually abbreviated as NV on bottles. You'll see this a lot with Champagne.

WORDS ABOUT
WINEMAKING

CARBONIC MACERATION: Sounds wildly complicated but is incredibly simple to understand. Whole bunches of uncrushed grapes are put into sealed containers that are pumped with CO_2. This kickstarts a fermentation that causes the grapes to split. A lot of colour but not much tannin is extracted, so it's a method used to make fruity wines like Beaujolais.

LEES CONTACT: Sounds like the makings of an infection, but is actually delicious. Lees are dead yeast cells left over from the fermentation process, which can add brilliant texture and biscuity notes to a wine. They're often filtered out, but some winemakers choose to leave the wine in contact with them, or 'sur lie', to add a complex texture. It's also common for sparkling wines like Champagne to be in contact with the lees for over a year, before they're fired out the bottle neck in a process called disgorgement.

LOW-INTERVENTION/NATURAL WINE: I prefer the term 'low-intervention' to 'natural wine' – a term that is widely used, but not at all legally defined, and which is a catch-all for anything that's been made with as little interference as possible. Don't get me wrong, I have no problem with the word natural, but to me, no wine is 'natural'. Bottles don't grow on trees. It is the winemaker's intuition and experience that conjures the grapes into something wonderful (or crap). Low intervention means the exact same thing, spanning organic and biodynamic practice. Herbicides and pesticides are avoided in the vineyard, and minimal sulphur is used in the cellar. The result? Wines that sing and dance on the palate. Many have observed how wines with little to no added sulphur are much more aromatic and fruit forward.

MACERATION: the technical term for 'skin contact', but it's not just used when making orange wine. Maceration is a stage in the winemaking process after the grapes are crushed and before they are pressed: the grape skins are left in contact with the juice for anything from a couple of minutes to several months. The longer the maceration, the more colour, texture and tannins extracted from the grapes.

MALOLACTIC FERMENTATION (MLF): This is a winemaking process that brings buttery flavours and an oily texture to a wine. It took me a while to wrap my head around, but basically, tart malic acid (which is naturally present in grapes) is converted to creamy-tasting lactic acid. It occurs making most red wines and some white wines, especially Chardonnay. And that, dear readers, is about as intellectual as this book gets.

TRADITIONAL METHOD (MÉTHODE TRADITIONNELLE): The classic way to make some of the world's most prestigious sparkling wines: Champagne, Crémant in all its delicious forms, Méthode Cap Classique, Franciacorta, Espumante and Cava are all made using the traditional method. Here, a base wine undergoes an initial fermentation, and then is put in bottles with a small amount of yeast and sugar (known as dosage) to start the second fermentation in the bottle. The bottle is then sealed with a cork.

IS IT A PLACE
OR IS IT A GRAPE?

Something of a wine 'cheat sheet', I anticipate these pages to be the ones most destined to become dog-eared. The pages you'll return to again and again, when faced with a particularly capacious bottle shop shelf, wine list or supermarket aisle.

When I was first starting out, I couldn't seem to find a catch-all place to quickly look up the name stated on a label. I didn't know whether I was looking at the name of a region or just a random grape I hadn't heard of yet. On a lot of French bottles, they don't include the name of the grape at all, and just state the name of the appellation, cru or vineyard. But how are you supposed to know what region that's in without an existent, expansive knowledge?

For myself, it was a long, arduous process of learning as I went. I learned by humbly making mistakes and asking questions (while still spending an embarrassing period of my life confusing Pouilly-Fuissé and Pouilly-Fumé). Hopefully, the following pages will take out all the guesswork from the bottles you're likely to come across. Please note that, for some non-French countries, I've used the word 'appellation' where I might have used 'commune' or 'winemaking area'. This is to simplify and give an idea of the scale of the areas – not big enough to be regions, but not small enough to be crus.

Abruzzo is a region in Italy
Aconcagua Valley is a region in Chile
Agiorgitko is a red grape
Aglianico is a red grape
Albariño/Alvarinho is a white grape
Alentejo is a region in Portugal
Aligoté is a white grape
Aloxe-Corton is an appellation in Burgundy
Alsace is a region in France
Anjou is a region in the Loire Valley
Assyrtiko is a white grape
Asti is an appellation in Italy
Auvergne is a region in France
Barolo is an appellation in Piedmont
Barbaresco is an appellation in Piedmont
Beaujolais is a region in France
Beaumes-de-Venise is an appellation in the Rhône Valley
Blaufränkisch is a red grape
Bobal is a red grape
Bordeaux is a region in France
Burgenland is a region in Austria
Burgundy is a region in France
Cabernet Franc is a red grape
Cabernet Sauvignon is a red grape
Cachapoal Valley is a region in Chile
Cahors is an appellation in France
Cairanne is an appellation in the Rhône Valley
Carménère is a red grape
Casablanca Valley is a region in Chile
Castilla y Léon is a region in Spain
Catalonia/Catalunya is a region in Spain
Cava is a sparkling wine produced in Catalonia/Catalunya
Central Otago is a region in New Zealand
Chablis is an appellation in Burgundy
Chambolle-Musigny is an appellation in Burgundy
Champagne is a region in France
Chardonnay is a white grape
Château-Grillet is an appellation in the Rhône Valley
Châteauneuf-du-Pape is an appellation in the Rhône Valley

Chenin Blanc is a white grape
Chianti is a region in Tuscany
Chinon is an appellation in the Loire Valley
Cinsault is a red grape
Clare Valley is a region in Australia
Colchagua Valley is a region in Chile
Condrieu is an appellation in the Rhône Valley
Coonawarra is a region in Australia
Cornas is an appellation in the Rhône Valley
Côte de Beaune is an area in Burgundy
Côte de Nuits is an area in Burgundy
Côte d'Or is an area in Burgundy
Côte-Rôtie is an appellation in the Rhône Valley
Côtes du Rhône is an appellation in the Rhône Valley
Côtes d'Auvergne is an appellation in the Loire Valley
Crozes-Hermitage is an appellation in the Rhône Valley
Curicó Valley is a region in Chile
Dão is a region in Portugal
Douro is a region in Portugal
Emilia-Romagna is a region in Italy
Entre-Deux-Mers is a region in Bordeaux
Garganega is a white grape
Gevrey-Chambertin is a village in Burgundy
Gigondas is an appellation in the Rhône Valley
Gisborne is a region in New Zealand
Givry is an appellation in Burgundy
Greco is a white grape
Grenache/Garnacha is a red grape
Grolleau is a red grape
Hautes-Côtes de Beaune is an appellation in Burgundy
Hautes-Côtes de Nuits is an appellation in Burgundy
Hawke's Bay is a region in New Zealand
Hermitage is an appellation in the Rhône Valley
Hunter Valley is a region in Australia
Itata Valley is a region in Chile
Jerez is a region in Spain
Kamptal is a region in Austria
Lambrusco is a red grape
Languedoc is a region in France

Libournais is an area in Bordeaux
Liguria is a region in Italy
Lirac is an appellation in the Rhône Valley
Loire Valley is a region in France
Lombardy is a region in Italy
Mâcon Villages is an appellation in Burgundy
Mâconnais is a region in Burgundy
Madeira is a region in Portugal
Maipo Valley is a region in Chile
Maipú is a region in Argentina
Malbec is a red grape
Margaret River is a region in Australia
Margaux is an appellation in Bordeaux
Marlborough is a region in New Zealand
Marsanne is a white grape
Martinborough is a region in New Zealand
Maule Valley is a region in Chile
Médoc is a region in Bordeaux
Melon de Bourgogne is a white grape
Mencía is a red grape
Mendoza is a region in Argentina
Menetou-Salon is an appellation in the Loire Valley
Mercurey is an appellation in Burgundy
Merlot is a red grape
Meursault is an appellation in Burgundy
Monastrell is a red grape
Morey-Saint-Denis is an appellation in Burgundy
Moschofilero is a white grape
Montagny is an appellation in Burgundy
Montepulciano is a red grape
Monterey is an appellation in California
Montrachet is an appellation in Burgundy
Moscatel/Moscato/Muscat is a white grape
Muscadet is an appellation in the Loire Valley
Napa Valley is an appellation in California
Nelson is a region in New Zealand
Nero d'Avola is a red grape
Nuits-Saint-Georges is an appellation in Burgundy
País is a red grape

Palomino is a white grape
Paso Robles is an appellation in California
Pauillac is an appellation in Bordeaux
Pedro Ximénez is a white grape
Pessac-Léognan is an appellation in Bordeaux
Petit Verdot is a red grape
Piedmont is a region in Italy
Pinot Meunier is a red grape
Pinot Noir is a red grape
Pinot Grigio/Pinot Gris is a white grape
Pinotage is a red grape
Pomerol is an appellation in Bordeaux
Pouilly-Fuissé is an appellation in Burgundy
Pouilly-Fumé is an appellation in the Loire Valley
Primitivo is a red grape
Prosecco is a wine produced in Veneto and Friuli Venezia Giulia
Provence is a region in France
Puligny-Montrachet is an appellation in Burgundy
Quincy is an appellation in the Loire Valley
Rasteau is an appellation in the Rhône Valley
Reuilly is an appellation in the Loire Valley
Rhône Valley is a region in France
Rías Baixas is a region in Spain
Ribera del Duero is a region in Spain
Riesling is a grape
Rioja is a region in Spain
Roussanne is a white grape
Roussillon is a region in France
Rutherglen is a region in Australia
Saint-Aubin is an appellation in Burgundy
Saint-Émilion is an appellation in Bordeaux
Saint-Estèphe is an appellation in Bordeaux
Saint-Péray is an appellation in the Rhône Valley
Saint-Pourçain is an appellation in the Loire Valley
Saint-Joseph is an appellation in the Rhône Valley
Saint-Julien is an appellation in Bordeaux
San Antonio Valley is an appellation in Chile
Sancerre is an appellation in the Loire Valley
Santa Barbara is an appellation in California

Santenay is an appellation in Burgundy
Saumur is a region in the Loire Valley
Sauternes is an appellation in Bordeaux
Sauvignon Blanc is a white grape
Savennières is an appellation in the Loire Valley
Savigny-lès-Beaune is an appellation in Burgundy
Sémillon is a white grape
Shiraz/Syrah is a red grape
Soave is a region in Italy
Sonoma is an appellation in California
Tarragona is a region in Spain
Tavel is an appellation in the Rhône Valley
Tempranillo/Tinta Roriz is a red grape
Tokaj is a region in Hungary
Touraine is a region in the Loire Valley
Touriga Nacional is a red grape
Tuscany is a region in Italy
Uco Valley is a region in Argentina
Umbria is a region in Italy
Vacueyras is an appellation in the Rhône Valley
Valdobbiadene is an area in Italy
Valpolicella is a region in Italy
Veneto is a region in Italy
Verdejo is a white grape
Verdicchio is a white grape
Vermentino is a white grape
Viré-Clessé is an appellation in Burgundy
Vosne-Romanée is an appellation in Burgundy
Vougeot is an appellation in Burgundy
Vouvray is an appellation in the Loire Valley
Vinho Verde is a region in Portugal
Vinsorbes is an appellation in the Rhône Valley
Wairarapa is a region in New Zealand
Willamette Valley is a region in Oregon
Xinomavro is a red grape
Yarra Valley is a region in Australia
Zweigelt is a red grape

LOVE

AND

SEX

A FIRST DATE
(THAT'S GOING WELL)

This book was born from the idea that you wouldn't order the same wine on two completely different dates. Sure, they've got a banging Clare Valley Riesling on the menu that you've been meaning to try, but what's the point if your date just called the waiter 'bossman'?

Wine isn't something we drink solely for personal pleasure (although there isn't a surface in my house that I haven't enjoyed a solo glass on). It's also something we discover and share in chosen moments, and I can scarcely think of a more deserving celebration than a date that's actually going well.

This is probably a second or third date, right? I've been known to ask a first date out to dinner (although I have since been told that this is a bit of a serial-killer move), but we can perhaps assume you're a little further along the line. You had one foot firmly on the ground initially, but tonight you're prepared to dive in headfirst and spend at least two hours together. And this is best lubricated with wine. You earnestly order by the glass at first. Conversation begins to flow as the wine list is handed over. Both of you reach out, and you feel the energy shift between your reaching palms.

'No, you choose. You said last week you'd read a brilliant book about situational wine pairing.' Oh, go on then. The tips of your fingers meet as the responsibility is passed. Hefty pages are flipped. A lower lip is gently bitten in anticipation.

Arched eyebrows flirt over bound paper (this last one doesn't really work if the wine list is on an iPad).

Are you already mentally booking your next date? Perhaps you're already fantasising about fucking on the sofa later on in the evening? This calls for a bottle of the good stuff.

BAROLO

Barolo is the answer. A smoky and elegant wine made from the Nebbiolo grape, hailing from foggy northern Italy. If you like Pinot Noir, then this is for you. I may be providing sordid details here on the bottle of wine I'd want on a date, but it's also the wine that Big Suze requests when she's out for dinner with Jeremy in season five of *Peep Show*. And he, the fool for her that he is, orders it ('A bottle of Barolo it is!') only to find out it's the most expensive on the menu. At £45. I, for one, would love to be able to get a good bottle of Barolo in a restaurant for £45, when I most recently saw a listing for £250. The things we do for love.

—

COLOUR:
red

NOTABLE GRAPES:
Nebbiolo

ON THE LABEL:
it will always say 'Barolo' on the label

CAN'T FIND IT? TRY THIS:
For something from the same grape, Barbaresco is also made in Piedmont and tends to be a little cheaper than Barolo, too.

A FIRST DATE
(THAT'S NOT GOING WELL)

'It's such a shame you enjoy drinking Prosecco,' the man across from me notes. 'A girl like you should really be drinking Champagne.' I think he thinks that's a compliment, but we're 15 minutes into the date and I've already decided that I never want to see him again. Earlier he referred to dating women as 'chasing tail'. The reaction to my order, however, is the final nail in the self-imposed cockblock coffin.

While I certainly wasn't about to deny my love of Champagne and, admittedly, it seems like a well-intended compliment written down, the way he pronounced 'Prosecco' with a bad imitation of an Essex accent was definitely indicative of something a little more grating, sexist and classist. Not exactly three boxes I want ticking on a first date.

So, what do you order, out of sheer politeness, of course, when you know you're going to find an excuse to leave in half an hour? The cab has already been ordered. You bribed your friend to call you with a faux emergency (her aunt's cat died). Time is of the essence, but you didn't come all this way for nothing.

You're certainly not ordering a bottle: then you're tossed on the horns of a shared bill situation, when you'd make a much hastier exit by paying for a single glass of something. Something that'll definitely be on the list. Something simple, yet reliable in style. If only there was such a wine. Oh wait, there is.

PROSECCO

It might seem like an arbitrary 'fuck you' to a man I dated several years ago (I wouldn't put it past me) but thinking about it, Prosecco is a genius option for a first date gone sour. The Italian fizz is almost always on by the glass, whether you're at a restaurant or wine bar – most pubs even stock it now. It's also often the cheapest by-the-glass option. Sparkling wine to toast the end of a calamitous rendezvous is the kind of delicious irony I can get behind. Cheers darling, better luck next time.

CAN'T FIND IT? TRY THIS:
If Prosecco isn't on the menu (although I can't imagine why it wouldn't be), then opt for some other fizz that's by the glass. A Col Fondo may be available, or opt for a gently effervescent pét-nat.

—

COLOUR:
white (sparkling)

NOTABLE
GRAPES:
predominantly
Glera, but up to 15
per cent of the wine
may be other
varieties such as
Verdiso or Pinot
Grigio

ON THE LABEL:
it will always say
'Prosecco' on the
label. Seeing
'Prosecco Superiore'
DOCG on the label
denotes a Prosecco
made in historic,
high-quality
vineyards

MEETING THE PARENTS

'I met someone, and things are getting serious. I watched them run up the stairs on all fours and I didn't get the ick. They have the password to my Now TV account. Now I'm meeting their family for the first time. What do I bring?'

I get this question more often than you'd think. It makes sense, from the perspective of a parent – a bottle of wine tells you all you need to know about a potential person-in-law. Looks expensive? Good career prospects. From an unfamiliar region? Knows their shit. Obviously bought last minute at a petrol station? At least they can drive.

It seems, in my own personal experience, that red wines are the safest option. They're more readily shared over an evening meal and look more costly. Just make sure the parents are drinkers first. A well-meaning ex brought round a bottle of red for my booze-averse parents, only for it to be politely shoved to the back of a cupboard, never to see daylight again. An apt premonition for the fate of the relationship? Perhaps. A great addition to my mother's casseroles? Absolutely.

CABERNET SAUVIGNON

We don't want to push the boat out too much here. I want to offer a suggestion that the older generation is going to be familiar with, feels a bit fancy and can be found in pretty much any bottle shop or supermarket. It's a bold, tannic variety that has a palate and a flavour profile that they probably already enjoy. So delicious, you'll forget all about your unpaid dentist bill and the ten points on your licence. Charming the in-laws has never been so effortless.

CAN'T FIND IT? TRY THIS:

If you're currently running up and down the wine aisle of the supermarket closest to your partner's childhood home and can't see a bottle marked 'Cabernet Sauvignon', don't fret. Some wines (especially French ones) don't mark the grape varieties on the label, rather the region the wine was made in. So, if you can see a 'Bordeaux Supérieur', 'Côtes de Bordeaux' from South Africa, Chile or Italy, these will have some Cab Sav in them. Go for that.

—

COLOUR:
red

NOTABLE REGIONS:
Bordeaux, Chile, South Australia, California, Tuscany, South Africa

ON THE LABEL:
you'll see 'New World' wines name the variety on the label, but in French regions like Bordeaux, you'll see the name of the château/appellation instead

DATE NIGHT
(YOU'RE GOING OUT)

I find first dates stressful. I find dates a year or so into a relationship rapturous. You can be as late as you want, there's no pressure for the food to be any good and they won't dump you if you turn up in battered Air Force 1s. All this, plus the fact you don't have to cook for yourself, makes for a heavenly evening.

Courtship, on the other hand, is a seedbed for wine anxiety.

I hated biting my tongue when a thoughtless (but totally fuckable) date would order the most eye-wateringly expensive bottle on the list in a bid to impress. But if you're into them, what can you do? As mood-killers go, nothing works like: 'Ahem, I'm actually doing an unpaid internship, so was thinking we could go by the glass and keep track of what we're spending?' It goes the other way too, where you're the totally fuckable party, but your oh-so-confident wine selection turns out to be undrinkable. You're too proud and they're too keen, so you end up exchanging watery smiles and wincing between sips. Horrific.

I shan't be recommending a wine for this scenario. It seems far more fitting to recommend a therapist. Instead, a wine suggestion for date night a year or so into a relationship. There is no mucking about in a steadfast partnership. You both know what the other likes and, more importantly, you both know what the other earns. If ever there was an argument for monogamy, wine list anxiety would most certainly be it.

WHITE BURGUNDY

Seductive, mouthwatering, what else could it be? White Burgundy (made from Chardonnay grapes) comes at all price points, so you're sure to find a bottle to fit the moment. The one drawback: it can be difficult to find on wine lists, on account of the fact that the bottle will never bear the word 'Chardonnay'. Instead, keep your eye out for key appellations. Some names likely to pop up in a wine list include Pouilly-Fuissé, Côte de Beaune, Savigny-lès-Beaune, Meursault, Santenay, Puligny-Montrachet, Saint-Aubin and Montagny (make sure it's a white wine, though, as some of these communes make white and red).

CAN'T FIND IT? TRY THIS:

If you're after something a little more saline, try Chablis, also made from Chardonnay, located at the top end of Burgundy. Other food-friendly Chardonnays can be found across the globe, you just need to know where to look. Seek out those from Chile, Tasmania, Oregon and Mendoza.

—

COLOUR:
white

NOTABLE GRAPES:
Chardonnay

ON THE LABEL:
no white Burgundy will say 'Chardonnay' on the label. Basic wines will state 'Bourgogne Blanc' (white Burgundy). Then, as quality rises, you will see the name of the appellation or the cru on the label.

DATE NIGHT
(YOU'RE STAYING IN)

I'm a total romantic. I dream of flowers, of truffles in a heart-shaped box, of a lover with joint-bank-account eyes. It's not very cool to be this type of person. It's something you usually grow out of when you turn 19, as you have your heart put in a washer-dryer by an empathy-deficient philosophy student that looks like he eats cigarettes. But delusional optimism remains my forté, especially when it comes to relationships.

It's important to make time for your significant other. A relatively easy way of doing this is the date night at home, when typically we'll find ourselves doing something completely uncharacteristic. For some of us, that might be making Bearnaise sauce or shaving the backs of our legs. For others, it might be changing out of pyjamas. Whatever extra mile you go to to make your partner/thruple/sugar daddy feel special, you have the luxury of planning in advance, so take some extra time in your local bottle shop to select the perfect wine. Something thrilling and tasty. Something special enough to pry your eyes from the latest Twitter meltdown and into the eyes of your beloved.

ZWEIGELT

I'm going to suggest Zweigelt. While it's becoming a little more common in supermarkets thanks to savvy wine buyers, you'll usually find the best Zweigelt in your local bottle shop. This Austrian grape has only been around for a little over a century, but it's already made an impression with red wine lovers. Brilliant, bursting with flavours of cherry, raspberry and liquorice, I usually pitch it as an Austrian Pinot Noir. It's effortlessly seductive and wonderful with food. I'll leave the rest up to you two/three.

CAN'T FIND IT? TRY THIS:
Pinot Noir will do nicely on this occasion, and if you've got the extra time, try and find something a bit more special. A bottle from Oregon, Central Otago or Burgundy ought to do the trick.

—

COLOUR:
red

NOTABLE REGIONS:
Austria

ON THE LABEL:
it will nearly always say 'Zweigelt' on the label

YOU'VE JUST HAD SEX

I want to be clear here, I'm not talking about shit sex. I'm not talking about they-texted-at-3am-and-you-came-running sex. I'm not even talking OK sex. I'm talking the kind of sex where you can't decide whether you want to giggle or thank God afterwards. Joyful sex. Not necessarily special occasion sex, but special sex nonetheless. Sex you ought to receive at least two business days' notice for, so, you know, you can plan to share a bottle of wine afterwards.

Whether you've already had a few or you're stone-cold sober, you definitely deserve a drink. And if this is something special, the person you're going to be with for the rest of your life (or at least the rest of your expensive holiday), it can't be a hastily poured tepid glass of water on the bedside table. It must, *must* be wine.

Post-coital drinks are something to be savoured, something that's chilling on ice as you bring up the average temperature of the room, like a big sexy iguana tank. Here's my suggestion for what you should savour together, toes touching, after the fact. I don't profess to be a serious wine writer, but if ever there was something to get me disowned from the wine industry, this page is it.

CHABLIS

Refreshing, lean and bone-dry, Chablis is my pick for some post-coital libation. Chablis is a region sandwiched between Champagne to the north and the southerly rest of Burgundy. There's generally less oak use, which makes the mineral, chalky quality of the wine shine. I figured you'd also need something, ahem, palate-cleansing, and Chablis' natural high acidity is fabulous for that. Here's to you both.

—

COLOUR:
white

NOTABLE GRAPES:
Chardonnay

ON THE LABEL:
it will always say 'Chablis' on the label

CAN'T FIND IT? TRY THIS:

If you just had sex with someone who doesn't like wine (though I can't imagine why you would), crack them open a Guinness. It's scientifically regarded as the perfect post-exercise drink, what with its abundance of minerals, vitamins, soluble fibre and prebiotics.

YOU'VE BEEN GHOSTED

The art of texting in a relationship's nascent days can be as delicate and easily ruined as single-ply toilet paper. I know those who have got it down to a precise art, setting egg timers to leave ample breathing room between correspondence, measuring the amount of perceived keenness to the nearest millimetre. The finest in their field maintain an intriguing spark without giving any mixed messages.

Ghosting, however, is about as definite a signal as you can get. The word entered the dictionary in 2017, presumably because it had become as common a modern occurrence as a cancelled flight or Claudia Winkleman presenting something excellent.

I remember the first time I got ghosted. At first, I didn't actually think I'd been ghosted. I genuinely thought their phone wasn't receiving texts or something terrible had happened to them. I texted again, and again. And again. I felt confused, and soon, my worry turned into uncertainty and self-loathing – I'm a nice enough person, how hard is it to say: 'I'm just not that into you?'

I'm now significantly more well-adjusted, but the reasons for ghosting remain a total headfuck. I'm sorry this happened to you, dear reader, let's get a glass of something special to clear your head, something that brings us such pleasure we have no spare moment to second-guess ourselves.

PLOUSSARD

The Jura is a winemaking region east of Burgundy and west of Switzerland, which produces wonderfully distinctive, surprising wines. It also has several indigenous varieties, including Ploussard. Ploussard is a very thin-skinned grape, which makes bright and ethereal red wines – it is often compared to Pinot – and rosé and sparkling wine are also made. For others, an exquisite expression of the Alpine climate; for me, a tonic for the soul – the seductive quality of Ploussard seems to ground me. The brain fog, the hazy static from the day lifts and I am alone with my wine. It's a wine that commands your attention and energy, and is far more deserving of it than someone who doesn't text back.

CAN'T FIND IT? TRY THIS:
If you'd like to try some other Jura wines, try Trousseau, a grape that produces forest fruit-scented, high-alcohol wines, often blended with Ploussard to add a bit of oomph. Besides Chardonnay, Savagnin is the hero white grape of the region, most famous for vin jaune – a nutty, sherry-esque wine that's matured under a layer of yeast known as the voile.

—

COLOUR:
red, rosé (or sparkling)

NOTABLE REGIONS:
Jura

ON THE LABEL:
may appear on the label as 'Poulsard', and may appear in wines labelled Arbois, Côtes du Jura, Crémant du Jura, L'Etoile and red or rosé Macvin du Jura.

THE END OF A RELATIONSHIP (YOU'RE GETTING DUMPED)

Do you prefer to do the dumping or to be dumped? It's an impossible would-you-rather to call (which of your testicles would you prefer to have dunked in hot oil?) but one we all come to blows with at one point or another. I've done both with varying degrees of success, composure and clothed-ness, but one thing is constant: I've always needed a strong drink afterwards.

Being dumped is never fun. Whether or not you see it coming, the feeling is often accompanied by the need to pick at every scab, uproot every put-to-bed argument and poke at every emotional bruise. It is my firm belief that you're entitled to one night where you do exactly this, post-breakup.

There are two things you will require. Firstly, friends: as acutely saccharine as it sounds, the best ones will drop everything for you. Secondly, a good bottle to ruminate over. While I'll never recommend drinking as the silver bullet solution (not the sole one, anyhow), you will need something to pour for your guests as they pile onto your three-seater sofa, where they smoke, shake their heads, and tell you how they 'actually never really liked them anyway'. In return for their services, you can provide the wine. Something brooding. Something red.

Over such a bottle, hours can be spent exploring and exhausting all avenues (with some dead ends and roundabouts, no doubt). And then, at some small hour of the morning, you'll realise all conversations meet at a mutual final realisation: that you're far better off without them.

BARBARESCO

I recommend Barbaresco for this. I received some bad news recently, and had a bottle of this in my cupboard for just such an emergency. The cherry notes of the Nebbiolo grape are uplifting, yet you can find stability in a subtle leathery earthiness. It's a little less common than other red wines, but one you're likely to find in your local (or online) independent bottle shop.

CAN'T FIND IT? TRY THIS:
Barolo is also made from Nebbiolo, but it is a little more expensive, so I'd reserve this for a jilted-at-the-altar situation. For another Italian red that balances smoky with fruity, try Barbera or Dolcetto, or seek out low-intervention styles of Cabernet Franc, Carignan and Grenache.

—

COLOUR:
red

NOTABLE GRAPES:
Nebbiolo

ON THE LABEL:
it will always say 'Barbaresco' on the label

THE END OF A RELATIONSHIP (YOU'RE DOING THE DUMPING)

In many ways, being the dumper is significantly worse than being the dumpee. There's the fine balance you have to strike between nauseating talk of friendship and the gut-wrenching bottom line that you would really rather never see them again. And, sometimes, you're the only one who knows that all of that is coming.

If a glass of wine is on the table, you've probably decided to have 'the talk' out in public. (In my opinion, this is psychotic, but sometimes neutral ground is called for.) Probably nowhere too fancy, you're definitely paying. After dragging your conscience through broken glass and getting a cool new rebrand as the worst person to have ever existed, the least you can do is pay the bill.

If you've ended up in the local bar, there are likely to be slim pickings, so you need something that's going to be found everywhere. Bonus points if it's not that high in ABV – boozy arguments never go well. It's easier to rip the band-aid off if you're not too drunk to say the word 'reciprocal'. Just take it slow, and only have the one glass. Oh God, they've started talking about the time you refused to make friends with the older couple on the cruise. You're probably going to be here for a while. Best get that drink in.

PINOT GRIGIO

A wine that I'm sure you're all familiar with, Pinot Grigio is known for a high acidity and palate-enlivening notes of lemon. Something so bright is sure to keep you alert during the deed. More importantly, it's always on by the glass at pretty much any bar or pub. Great for a swift drink and an even swifter exit.

It's also worth nothing that this is the same grape as Pinot Gris, but when made in France instead of Italy, it yields altogether a different style with notes of flowers and orchard fruit.

CAN'T FIND IT? TRY THIS:

The reasons I gave above for choosing a Pinot Grigio (it's both cheap and ubiquitous) were not ones rooted in gastronomy. They were, however, rooted in flawless logic. This is practical drinking at its finest. If there's none on the menu, opt for the other white wines by the glass. For those of you seeking alternatives based on flavour profile, fine. Try Chardonnay, Albariño, Fiano or Assyrtiko.

—

COLOUR:
white

NOTABLE REGIONS:
Italy

ON THE LABEL:
it will nearly always say 'Pinot Grigio' on the label

YOU'VE JUST GOT ENGAGED

Congratulations! If you're reading this page, you've either already popped the question or you're looking to these pages for some romantic inspiration. This is a story you will inevitably retell to every family member/friend/passerby/masseuse from this day forward, so you'd better toast it with something good.

I'm going to suggest a wine for proposals that take place at home, not because the very idea of a public proposal makes my toes curl (major kudos to any readers brave enough to do this), but because you can have more of a say on what wine you're going to open after. Don't get swept up in them saying yes and dropping £200 on a bottle of Champagne. The saving starts now.

It is remarkable how taste and smell are so inexorably linked to memory. It's why the smell of highlighters transports you back to revising for exams, or a certain brand of vodka incites an instant psychic flashback to a ruinous night. It's also why wine tasting can be so subjective: to you, a wine may totally smack of the cantaloupe melons you enjoyed as a child, to someone else, another thing entirely.

Basically, I'm trying to say that this wine needs to make an impression. It needs to be something unique that will take you back to this treasured moment.

Oh, and if it's a home proposal, it can't be Champagne. You want it to be ice cold once they say yes, right? Do you have a

secret fridge? No? Then it can't be Champagne. If you're not habitually fancy drinkers, nothing arouses suspicion like a bottle of Blanc de Blancs in the fridge door. There's nothing like an accusatory, 'Babe . . . what's this for?' to throw a vinous spanner in the works. Get something interesting under the guise of 'trying something new' and they're none the wiser. Follow me for more gaslighting tips.

SPARKLING VOUVRAY

So as not to alert suspicions, I'm going to suggest sparkling Vouvray, a wine made in the Loire Valley from the region's star grape, Chenin Blanc. You can get it dry or slightly sweet, depending on what kind of wines you both like. Expect totally unmistakable notes of pear, melon and apple, with gorgeous honeysuckle too. If you've opted for a sweeter wine, you'll get ginger and honey from any presence of noble rot.

CAN'T FIND IT? TRY THIS:
Crémant d'Alsace (sparkling wine from Alsace) is an equally impactful fizz. It's a blend of many grapes, including the aromatic varieties of Riesling, Pinot Gris and Pinot Noir, among others. It's likely to be a bit friendlier to your wallet too if you've already sold all your belongings to pay for a ring. If you *must* get Champagne, opt for something opulent and biscuity that's undergone a bit of lees-ageing or spent a fair bit of time in the bottle. This important moment is worthy of the good stuff.

—

COLOUR:
white (sparkling)

NOTABLE GRAPES:
Chenin Blanc

ON THE LABEL:
it will nearly always say 'Méthode Traditionnelle' on the label. Less often, you'll see 'Mousseaux', which means 'frothy'. 'Brut' means the wine will be bone-dry, whereas 'Demi-Sec' means it will be a little sweet

WEDDINGS

Unoriginal observation warning: I'm now at the stage when *everyone* seems to be getting engaged or married. An inescapable tidal wave of other people's happiness.

One thing I've ascertained from the few weddings I've attended is the mad stuff the happy couple is willing to spend money on. You chat with the mother-of-the-bride on the tastefulness and originality of the taco stand and the four-legged ring bearer. You smile with impeccable mirth as the bride and groom begin their 'surprise' choreographed first dance with a troupe of professional dancers.

I'm of the firm belief that it's your God-given right to submit your friends and family to whatever weird shit you're into for one day. There are all manner of things you can spend your hard-earned money on, but one of these things is, unless your religion lets you off the hook, booze. From the toast to the meal to the contentious issue of the open bar, costs inescapably rise. If you're looking for inspiration for your wedding wines, or hacks to keep costs down, read on.

— FOR THE TOAST

When we consider what it is that we *actually* want from a toast, it's likely the wine that we pore over the most. Whether you're having an intimate affair in a local pub or a gargantuan fuck-off wedding in the heel of Italy complete with F-list celebrity officiator, the one thing they'll have in common is at least one toast. It underlines the importance of the day, as much there for decoration as it is the vibe. It's the focal point of a wedding's pivotal moments, so needs to be pretty as well as tasty.

BLANC DE BLANCS

I can't think of having anything else other than Champagne for my wedding day, although I feel this statement may age poorly in the wake of this cost-of-living crisis, meaning I'm far more likely to be toasting my big day with a can of Ting. But Blanc de Blancs (Champagne that's 100% Chardonnay), with its fine stream of bubbles, pale straw colour and crowd-pleasing notes of citrus and pastry, is a brilliant option.

CAN'T FIND IT? TRY THIS:

If Blanc de Blancs is out of your budget, seek out Méthode Cap Classique: South Africa's flagship sparkling wine. It's made using the exact same method as Champagne, but you'll find it's way better value (and I doubt the in-laws will be able to taste the difference). South Africa's white sparkling wines are usually made from Chenin Blanc or Chardonnay, and offer similar creamy textures, enlivened by green apple and notes of brioche from lees-ageing.

—

COLOUR:
white (sparkling)

NOTABLE GRAPES:
Chardonnay

ON THE LABEL:
some Champagnes will say 'Blanc de Blancs' on the label, but some won't, even if they're 100% Chardonnay. It's best to look on the back of the bottle to see if there's a blend breakdown

— FOR THE MEAL

As much as this isn't a food and wine pairing book, dining is perhaps wine's most essential experience. The wedding meal, regardless of how big or small it may be, deserves a good accompaniment, and one that can be obtained at a variety of price points.

RED BURGUNDY

On a personal note, there's not really a time where I don't want a glass of red Burgundy. So special is it to me, that I think even drinking it at my wedding meal, the novelty will not wear off. Red Burgundy is 100% Pinot Noir, and a breadth of delicious styles (and price tags) can be offered across the region. For the budget-conscious, fruity, easy-drinking 'Bourgogne Rouge' will fit the bill. For the deep-pocketed, seek out powerful Gevrey-Chambertin or perfumed Volnay (if you have the wedding budget for this, call me if it doesn't work out).

CAN'T FIND IT? TRY THIS:

For something that offers the food-friendliness and sumptuous fruit for über-quaffing, try Pinot from other winemaking regions: New Zealand, Oregon, Germany and Austria will definitely fit the bill. Or, if you must go French, there is inexpensive Pinot to be found across the country, and Beaujolais is always a good idea.

—

COLOUR:
red

NOTABLE GRAPES:
Pinot Noir

ON THE LABEL:
no red Burgundy will say 'Pinot Noir' on the label. Basic wines will state 'Bourgogne Rouge' (red Burgundy) on the label. Then, as quality rises, you will see the name of the appellation or the cru on the label, such as Givry-Chambertin or Romanée-Conti, respectively

—FOR THE OPEN BAR

'Look, if I'm going to have to order 50 bottles of it, it had better be cheap' – so generously stated one of my wedding-planning friends. Scrooge-like though it may seem, I have to agree. Unless you're marrying a Viscount who also happens to own the patent for Velcro, an open bar gets bloody expensive. Thankfully, your partner, their family and your friends are also (usually) the first to understand that you have a budget. So, what you need is another type of marriage: one that joins value and quality in the holiest of matrimonies. With this equation nailed, guests will be so well watered they'll scarcely be able to remember who's getting married, let alone what they're drinking.

ALIGOTÉ

When the day comes, I shall be sipping Aligoté all evening. It's infamously known as the unappreciated bastard white grape of Burgundy, while Chardonnay is the golden child that plays the cello. With bright citrus and a salinity that can resemble Cornish butter, Aligoté is a happy medium between the quality offered by a prestigious appellation and the value to be found in wines that fly a little more under the radar. Plus, you'll definitely want a white wine in your glass as things get a little more rowdy. Event hire glasses tend to have wider rims, and nothing forebodes a doomed marriage like a wedding dress stained with Rioja.

CAN'T FIND IT? TRY THIS:
Other white wines from Burgundy will work just as well. You'll find value in the Mâconnais, the most southerly region of Burgundy, so taste a few wines that mention 'Mâcon-Villages' on the label.

—

COLOUR:
white

NOTABLE REGIONS:
Burgundy

ON THE LABEL:
it will nearly always say 'Aligoté' on the label

— FOR A GIFT

I think wine is one of the most brilliant gifts you can buy a newlywed couple. A garlic mincer is sure to find its way to the bottom of the third kitchen drawer, but a bottle of wine! If they got engaged in the summer, gift them a wine that was made from grapes that were ripening as someone was working up the courage to pop the question. Or buy it a little later, so that the vintage can mark the year of their marriage. Or, even better, splash out on a case of something age-worthy, and they can open a bottle on their one-, two-, five- and ten-year anniversaries.

RIESLING

Thoroughly inspired by a colleague who did exactly the same, I recommend Riesling as a wedding gift. Riesling ranges from bone-dry to super-sweet. Both styles age impeccably, developing from citrus and apple to notes of honey, petrol (in a good way), beeswax, spice and toast as well. For me, there are few bottles that age as excitingly as a Riesling, and it'll make a fab addition to the cellar of the betrothed.

CAN'T FIND IT? TRY THIS:

There are loads of wines with 10 or even 20 years of ageing potential. Some I recommend are wines made from Nebbiolo (like Barolo or Barbaresco), red wines from Tuscany, and Rioja (in both colours). You can also get some wines 'en primeur', where you buy directly from the producer the year they're released at their cheapest. They won't be ready right away, but they'll be singing a few years later.

—

COLOUR:
white

NOTABLE REGIONS:
Mosel, Rheingau, Hungary, Austria, New Zealand, United States, Canada

ON THE LABEL:
the word 'Riesling' is unlikely to feature on a German bottle. Instead, keep an eye out for the elongated bottle shape and the different Riesling sweetness designations: Kabinett, Spätlese, Auslese, Beerenauslese, Trockenbeerenauslese and Eiswein

IT'S YOUR ANNIVERSARY

A long relationship is by no means the only measure of its quality but, by God, does it mean you know them well. It's all well and good to feel loved and told you're brilliant and sexy, but it is an entirely different, very vital, thing to have the angular, rotting parts of our personalities acknowledged alongside this. We reveal so very much of ourselves to our partner, and they're there, with saint-like patience, to hear you out, plot with you or tell you you're being a dick. The good ones will do so for decades. What I'm trying to say is, you therefore can't uncork any old plonk for an anniversary. It's just not on.

The cool thing to do is to open a bottle from the same vintage as the year you got married. The grapes could have been fattening under the sun, picked for the harvest, or blended into a wine when you were saying your vows. It's a romantic notion, but the better you are at staying together, the more grievous the gesture will be on the shared bank account.

By the above logic, a good anniversary wine needs to be age-worthy, as well as delicious whether it's one or ten years old. If you're at two years, it needs to be something you're likely to find in your local bottle shop. If you're at ten, something you can seek out especially, but isn't as dear as some fine wine regions tend to be. If you've surpassed 20 years, you don't deserve a bottle of wine, you deserve a fucking trophy.

CHÂTEAUNEUF-DU-PAPE

The Châteauneuf-du-Pape appellation allows for the production of red and white wines, but for this we'll be focusing on its reds, which are significantly more age-worthy (up to 20 years, for some producers). A classic Châteauneuf will be bursting with dark plum notes and other red fruit, with elegant top notes of dried Provençal herbs and leather. This is a reliably polished wine that you can pick up at your local independent bottle shop with a few years of bottle age, but you can also find online with a decade of bottle ageing, and for not as much as its more costly Rhône neighbours.

CAN'T FIND IT? TRY THIS:
Nearby Côtes du Rhône has a similar, if simpler, flavour profile, but the best will last up to around a decade. Other age-worthy red wines include those made from the Nebbiolo grape (like Barolo and Barbaresco), red Rioja, Pinot Noir (especially from Burgundy) and Cabernet Sauvignon-based wines. If you're after a white wine, Riesling is another great option – some of these can age for over 20 years, as can white Rioja. (If you want a nifty idea on what to buy a just-married couple, refer to the wedding section on page 62).

—

COLOUR:
red

NOTABLE GRAPES:
13 varieties are permitted, including Grenache Noir, Syrah, Mourvèdre and Cinsault

ON THE LABEL:
it will always say 'Châteauneuf-du-Pape' on the label

YOU'VE JUST FINALISED A DIVORCE

Not to tempt fate, but I think I'd make a brilliant ex-wife. So many of the things that I already love – wearing black, smoking heavily, complaining about exes – make me an ideal candidate for the position, should one become available. The divorce rate still lingers at around 50%, so it's an eventuality we may need to prepare ourselves for. For those of us that marry, a 50% chance at happiness, but also a 50% chance we'll have to divvy up the loot, the kids and the pets (this is why I think it's best to have two of everything).

I'm at the stage of life where divorces are few and far between, but I have been to one divorce party, held in a wine bar. We were all encouraged to wear black to signify the end of a huge part of the divorcee's life, but it was an incredibly joyous affair. Wine was shared by the bucketload. Cigarettes were shared outside in the cold as the sun set and the chapter closed. Here's to new beginnings. You need something to toast to that. You only have a first divorce once.

BARBERA

You need something seductive and delicious as you grow into your power. Something to draw a line under the whole nasty affair, and beckon in your new-found freedom. There's something about Barbera that gets my pleasure receptors firing on all cylinders. The grape is the most widely planted in the regions of Asti and Alba. Look out for Barbera d'Alba DOC and Barbera d'Asti DOCG for some truly delicious examples. In their youth, Barbera wines are chock-full of plum and cherries, with a top note of pepper. Barrel-aged Barbera will yield a much more spicy expression.

CAN'T FIND IT? TRY THIS:
Nebbiolo is the other star grape of northern Italy, known widely for producing the sainted Barolo and Barbaresco wines. These are just as deep and a little more perfumed, plus a little more expensive. But if your budget allows for it, go for it.

—

COLOUR:
red

NOTABLE REGIONS:
Italy, United States, Australia and Argentina

ON THE LABEL:
it will always say 'Barbera' on the label, but keep an eye out for it hidden alongside the names of Italian regions, such as Barbera d'Asti, or Barbera d'Alba

A

DAY

OUT

BARBECUES

Every year, around the beginning of June, I brace myself for the barbecue DMs. They arrive in their droves, thirsty and with awful tanlines, and they all say something to the effect of: 'Hannah, I've been invited to a barbecue, what on earth do I bring?' I get the panic. The arrival of the barbecue signifies the start of summer, personified by the invite from a friend of a friend who has a garden. For those of you who live in London, this is the equivalent of knowing someone who shits gold eggs.

The prognosis is simple: you'll want to walk in with something that quenches the thirst but also matches with a relatively unknown menu. Classy but cautious. You'll want something to win the respect of the homeowner (the possibility of further garden invites hangs in the balance), but you don't want to fork out for something that invariably finds itself shoved in the ice cooler with the Peronis. I've been there – a bottle of premier cru Chablis looks far less impressive after its label has been soaked off.

CÔTES DU RHÔNE

No matter what's being thrown on the barbecue, a red Côtes du Rhône will match those charred, smoky flavours, meat and veggies alike, but it's also just as delicious served on its own. Classically, it's a little peppery, with loads of red fruit. Modern expressions lean towards a fresh, fruity style – ideal for summer quaffing that expends little brain energy. You'll be garden guy's new best friend – further outdoor excursions, here we come.

CAN'T FIND IT? TRY THIS:
Grenache, Syrah or Cinsault – these are the constituent parts of a Côtes du Rhône, but they work just as well on their own. Go for Grenache for something a little lighter, Syrah for something spicy and Cinsault for a punchy, fruity sip. For something bigger and bolder, a Primitivo or Zinfandel will do the trick.

—

COLOUR:
red, white and rosé

NOTABLE REGIONS:
Rhône Valley

ON THE LABEL:
you'll always see the words 'Côtes du Rhône' on a bottle of Côtes du Rhône, plus the name of the village if it's a Côtes du Rhône with a named village (a step above a 'Côtes du Rhône Villages', confusingly)

PICNICS (IT'S WARM)

Picnics: they're a good idea until they aren't. You've had your first few weeks of sunshine, so you're starting to feel confident about the return of summer. 'Hey, guys, fancy a picnic?' The pin is pulled and the grenade is thrown into the group chat, who run with it like they've never been on a picnic in their lives: Frankie will bring the sausage rolls, Oliver will bring the nibbly bits, which leaves you – as the designated expert – to sort the wine.

But what to bring? Something to suit the summer, so nothing too tannic or serious, obviously, but it'll need to stand up to the gentle, salty flavour of charcuterie and olives. Ahead of the inevitable realisation that you've picked a spot too exposed to the sun at high noon, and with nowhere left to go, you'll also need a wine to quench your thirst.

—
COLOUR:
pink

NOTABLE
REGIONS:
Loire Valley, Tuscany

ON THE LABEL:
some rosé wines
may say 'Cabernet
Franc' on the label,
but in French
regions such as the
Loire, they will name
the appellation
instead (head to
page 24 to see if the
name on the bottle
is an appellation)

CABERNET FRANC ROSÉ

You may have had the pleasure of having
Cabernet Franc, but the rosé it yields – most
commonly from the Loire in France – makes
for perfect picnic sipping. A pronounced
perfume of blackcurrants and raspberries is
elevated by a subtle vegetal edge, making it an
ideal match for any nibbly bits. Cabernet
Franc never misses a moment to unexpectedly
flourish, especially when the sun's out.

CAN'T FIND IT? TRY THIS:

Honestly? I think Cabernet Franc in its more
customary form would also be pretty good. It's
a red wine that sings when chilled. Youthful,
ready-to-drink versions even more so. Expect
even more intense notes of raspberry and
strawberry, with a hint of steminess.

PICNICS (IT'S COLD)

Who said eating outside had to be a pleasurable experience?

The thought of dining al fresco is a thoroughly romantic one. It always looks so much better in our heads ('of course I'd love to come for a drink in the park!'), images abounding of reclining on chequered picnic blankets. Your friends are all laughing, sipping rosé and, for some reason, wearing berets. Then you remember that you live in the shit part of Europe that no one likes, least of all Mother Nature.

Look, if it's cold outside and you're selecting a wine to drink outside, the first thing that comes to mind is a white, right? Drinking rosé when it looks like the heavens may open is a tad too tongue-in-cheek (nobody will be around to see your brilliantly ironic joke), and reds are for indoors, surely?

I'm going to put forward another proposal. You're going to put your sensible, moth-eaten coat on, you're going to get two of your finest plastic IKEA tumblers that you bought for a barbecue you've never had, and you're going to grab a bottle of red from your wine rack. One that sings in the cold and warms your insides so generously you'd barely notice if your fingers started to fall off.

BEAUJOLAIS

Made from 100% Gamay, the exuberance of Beaujolais is sure to enliven the gloomiest park bench. From a region just south of Burgundy, the wine comes in a variety of styles, but what unites them are the lovely, cheerful fruit-forward flavours of cherry, violet and – if you're sipping some Beaujolais Nouveau – youthful notes of banana, bubblegum and kirsch.

CAN'T FIND IT? TRY THIS:

There are many other red wines that taste great when chilled, just make sure you choose ones that are designed to be drunk young, lest you encounter an age-old foe: overly chilled, very tannic wine. Overly chilling a tannic wine such as a robust style of Bordeaux or Chianti would only further enhance the tannins and smother the fruit, leaving you with an acerbic mouthfeel that I can only imagine tastes like weedkiller. To avoid this fate, try lighter styles of Pinot Noir, Cabernet Franc and sparkling reds like Lambrusco.

—

COLOUR:
mainly red, with some white and rosé

NOTABLE GRAPES:
Gamay

ON THE LABEL:
some Beaujolais wines will say 'Beaujolais' or 'Beaujolais Villages' on the label. Where the wine is from a named cru – such as Fleurie or Moulin-à-Vent – the bottle will say the cru's name instead (head to page 24 to see if the name on the bottle is a cru)

YOU'RE AT A BOOZY BRUNCH

Participating in a boozy brunch isn't yet a competitive sport, but there are definitely those who treat it like it is. They organise the girlies in the group chat like Churchill in the war rooms. They spend the same amount of time getting ready as is advisable to spend on open-heart surgery. And, of course, they are sure to drink a medically inadvisable amount of wine.

Prosecco is undoubtedly the first drink that comes to mind when considering the boozy brunch, whether atrociously ill-fated or miraculously well-behaved. But, allow me to sidestep the obvious option. I'm sure you've picked up this book to learn something new, and it's not exactly an industry secret that Prosecco + brunch = good (although you can read a little bit about Prosecco on page 36).

No, instead I'm going to provide an alternative for if you're planning a boozy brunch at home, but we're not going to stray too far from the blueprint. It's the ambrosia of the British hun, a recession-proof way to drink fabulously. And I've long been an advocate for the life-affirming effect of bubbles. If it ain't flat, don't fix it.

—

COLOUR:
white (sparkling)

NOTABLE
GRAPES:
Chardonnay, Pinot
Nero (Pinot Noir)
and Pinot Bianco
(Pinot Blanc). Greco
is also permitted in
wines from Greco di
Tufo

ON THE LABEL:
it will always say
'Metodo Classico' on
the label

METODO CLASSICO

Often made in the same region as Prosecco, Metodo Classico is essentially the same thing as Méthode Traditionnelle, the sparkling winemaking method used to make Champagne. When made with Chardonnay, Pinot Nero and Pinot Bianco, you get notes of apple and pear and brioche and toast from the lees-ageing.

CAN'T FIND IT? TRY THIS:
Lambrusco is a great shout here. It's just as cost-effective and inspires a similar vivifying joy (more on that on page 114). Spumante deserves a special mention. Literally translating to 'fizzy wine', this is a catch-all term for sparkling wine made anywhere in Italy and from any grape variety. Naturally, this means that quality will vary, so be sure to do some research before buying a bottle.

DRINKING BY THE SEA
(YOU'RE IN THE UK)

Surrounding Brexit Island, the body of land formerly known as the United Kingdom, is more coastline than we know what to do with. There's a thing in the industry known as 'seasonal drinking', but so much of our lives are dictated by the weather in the UK, it feels far less of a seasonal whim and more of an acute need to get our bloody money's worth while the sun's out.

The British seaside is something we are incredibly lucky to have, but because of its myriad contradictions, we just don't appreciate it. It is inconsistently beautiful. Its cliff faces are shocking white but its pebble beaches are unforgiving on drunken feet. News outlets run annual items on the blistered bodies that visit in summer but focus on what they leave behind.

There's something so dissatisfactory yet optimistic about the British seaside, whatever the time of year, whether your bag of chips weeps grease in the sun or nips your freezing fingers as steam pours from your mouth. For such occasions, a glass of wine to bring the chips to a palatable temperature is advised, plus something that'll evoke all the freshness of a salty seaside walk.

CHENIN BLANC

From the softly bruised apples of Saumur to the rich (and increasingly subtle) wines from South Africa, Chenin Blanc is a super-versatile grape with a range to suit most people's tastes. It's originally from the Loire Valley, which yields many fine examples, but has found a second home in South Africa. Either will do perfectly.

CAN'T FIND IT? TRY THIS:

Let's not go too mad here, I'm definitely not going to recommend anything too fancy. Be honest, the bottle you're probably necking has either already gone warm or is contributing to an ever-thickening wine jacket. Other aromatic white wines that might fit the bill include Sauvignon Blanc, Pinot Grigio and Chardonnay – simples.

—

COLOUR:
white

NOTABLE REGIONS:
Loire Valley, South Africa

ON THE LABEL:
'New World' countries will nearly always say 'Chenin Blanc' on the label. Most wines from Bordeaux or the Loire Valley, will only state the appellation or the châteaux on the label (head to page 24 to see if the name on the bottle is an appellation)

PUBLIC TRANSPORT

Let's talk boozing in public. Sometimes the only thing that gets you through the working day is the promise of a good drink. While everybody else in the office is faxing and heading into their four o'clocks, I dream of stiff martinis and undulating pours of red wine. Alcoholic or otherwise, there's something endlessly cathartic about that first drink. It is a conquest embodied by the smug face of the triumphant sip in a Coca-Cola advert.

But sometimes, the minutiae of life admin gets in the way of that fantasy. We have to head home to accept an Asos parcel or walk a dog with Oedipal attachment issues. Thus, the after-work beverage has to be consumed en route. It's something everybody does. Our ears twitch with thirst as we hear the click of an opening can. Our collective delight peaks when we catch a celebrity or politician downing a quick bev on a plane, train or automobile.

In recent years, tinned drinks – and especially tinned wine – have become incredibly popular. It's the perfect size to drink in one go, and the steely cans keep the wine inside satisfyingly cool. Increasingly, there are finer wines available in cans (stuff like orange wine and Zweigelt, which you should seek out in advance, stuff your fridge with and thank me later), but if you're about to hop on a delayed train, you must reach for something more readily available.

SAUVIGNON BLANC

I went into a supermarket in every London train station I travel through, and the one thing that all of them had nestled on their grab-n-go shelves was tinned Sauvignon Blanc. It's a dry, aromatic wine we're all familiar with, the most loved ones being from New Zealand and France. It translates well into a can: it's nice and light, it's crisp, it's best served chilled. A cool full stop to a hectic day.

CAN'T FIND IT? TRY THIS:
Bright, fresh Pinot Grigio also works well in a can, and was the second-most available wine I saw in my tour of train stations. If your boozy commute could use a touch more class, canned rosé is also on the up.

—

COLOUR:
white

NOTABLE REGIONS:
New Zealand, Bordeaux, Loire Valley, Chile, South Africa

ON THE LABEL:
'New World' countries will nearly always say 'Sauvignon Blanc' on the label. In French regions such as the Loire, they will name the appellation instead. When it's part of a Bordeaux blend, it will only state the appellation or châteaux

YOU'RE AT A PUB

Hi there, and welcome. I know a lot of you will have made a beeline to this page when you bought this book. Just how do you navigate this minefield of shit wine? I've taken it upon myself to do the research, inspecting the wine list (although I fear 'list' may be an altogether far too generous description) of every chain pub I've been into in the last year.

There are many independent pubs with fabulous wine lists, built lovingly by dedicated owners and publicans. This page isn't for those places, where you'll no doubt find something brilliant to sip. Many of the chain establishments are yet to catch up. This page is advice for *those* places.

At these pubs, the pickings are slim, and we don't want to ask the well-meaning landlord exactly what he means when he says he has 'red or white'. Most of the time, we just end up having a beer. But what about when you don't want a beer? What if you are dead set on having wine, you just want one that tastes good?

The fact is: pubs are part of our DNA. They are as British as baked beans and not going to therapy. They are also the first place that many of us unknowingly start our wine journeys. Many a trembly voiced first wine order has taken place in a British pub, for those of us who aren't lucky enough to have parents with cellars full of Lafite. Here's how to hack the pub wine list.

— YOU'RE INDOORS

Many of the pubs I grew up near to did not have the luxury of a beer garden. They were cramped, carpeted places with low wooden beams and ruddy, friendly faces. They were places to hide in after a particularly long walk or to reconvene with old school friends at Christmastime. Places that come into their own in the winter months, with a real fire and a packet of cheese and onion crisps to split open. When you're indoors, you require something similarly festive and warming.

MERLOT

What puts me off the most in cheap pub wine is the sugar content. Red comes in at around 0.9g of sugar per serving, whereas white wine can be around 1.4g. So, for my pub order, I often go for a red. And Merlot was by far the most popular red I found in the places I visited. Plummy, ripe Merlot, from the Old and New Worlds.

CAN'T FIND IT? TRY THIS:
I also encountered many Malbecs on my journey around the country's pubs. A similarly smooth, jammy wine with notes ranging from raspberry to blackberry, depending on how hot the climate is.

—

COLOUR:
red

NOTABLE REGIONS:
Bordeaux, California, Chile, Australia, Hungary

ON THE LABEL:
'New World' countries will nearly always say 'Merlot' on the label. Most wines from Bordeaux, where it's mixed into a blend, will only state the appellation or châteaux

— YOU'RE OUTDOORS

The beer garden is an altogether different beast. It's more sociable, busier, and scientifically ten times more likely to result in a Deliveroo McDonald's at 11am the next day. There's still a way to dodge overly sugary wines here – you just need to seek out a wine with a bracing acidity to cut through the noise.

WHITE RIOJA

Each time I've had a white Rioja at a chain pub, it's been pretty good. Lemon, herbs, and round melon are balanced by a delicate minerality. The key here is quality: in order to put the words 'white Rioja' on a label, the wine has to have met a certain level of quality, oak ageing and bottle ageing.

CAN'T FIND IT? TRY THIS:
My next suggestion would be a standard Sauvignon Blanc, another white wine that the pub is sure to have. If they don't, just have a beer.

—

COLOUR :
white

NOTABLE GRAPES:
Viura (minimum 51%), Malvasia, Tempranillo Blanco, Garnacha Blanca

ON THE LABEL:
it will always say 'Rioja' or 'Rioja Blanco' on the label

BIRTHDAY LUNCH (IT'S YOURS)

Not to out myself as the poster girl of social neurosis, but I feel like this book needs a page on how to navigate your own birthday. You would have thought that it was the one time of the year you could let go, basking in the adoration of your loved ones/admirers. But here you are on this page, presumably because you find birthdays just as stressful as I do, and clutch at any literary guidance on how to act like a normal human being.

The most common occurrence, I reckon, unless you're lucky enough to have the type of friends who are willing to drop £40 each on a meal, is a lunch around yours. Hosting, in and of itself, is a migraine-inducing affair, and that's before you have to figure out what to do with your face when everyone is singing 'Happy Birthday'. Hint: don't pull an expression as if both your boyfriends just walked through the door.

As the birthday boy/girl/person, you definitely shouldn't be bringing the best bottle to your own party, but it's a nice gesture to have something already chilled in the fridge to uncork (on unscrew) as everyone else arrives with warm bottles of white and shaken-up fizz. Pour, sit back, and if you have to touch a bottle for the rest of the day, get yourself some new friends.

—

COLOUR:
white

NOTABLE
REGIONS :
Loire Valley

NOTABLE
GRAPES:
Melon de
Bourgogne

ON THE LABEL:
it will always say
'Muscadet' on the
label

MUSCADET

Made from a grape called Melon de Bourgogne, Muscadet is a white wine made in the west of the Loire Valley, close to the Atlantic coast. The wines are bulked up by extended time on lees and tend to be saline and citrusy. Muscadet is the generic appellation, but it contains three sub-appellations: Muscadet-Sèvre et Maine, which produces 80% of wine in the region, Muscadet-Coteaux de la Loire and Muscadet-Côtes de Grandlieu – keep an eye out for these on the label. They're easily picked up in most supermarkets or bottle shops.

CAN'T FIND IT? TRY THIS:

For other easy-going white wines (that don't entail paying more than £15 on your birthday), look for youthful examples of Verdicchio, white Côtes du Rhône, Picpoul de Pinet and white Rioja.

BIRTHDAY LUNCH
(IT'S SOMEONE ELSE'S)

And now, the other side of the looking glass: a birthday that isn't yours. They're easier to enjoy, and whether it's a BYOB at your local curry house or an intimate lunch round theirs (see page 86 for if it's round yours), it's common courtesy to bring something along to contribute to the merriment of the gathering.

Etiquette professionals will not hesitate to peer over their voluminous cravat and tell you how wrong it is to bring a bottle round to someone's house if you don't know their specific tastes in wine. I call BS, and I'd like to ask them when ordinary people have a conversation about what percentage of Sémillon they favour in their white Bordeaux. Hell, I don't even know what kind of wine my closest friend likes, but isn't it more fun to explore this together? Drinking wine in everyday environments is how we learn about wine; it's how we discover what kind of wine we like. The wine is there, but it's by no means the focal point of the celebrations.

The bottle in question has got to be special, but not so special that it's going to bankrupt you every time a friend has a birthday. Nothing screams 'budgeting is a language I never learned to speak' like turning up to the lunch with a bottle of Roederer and then drinking Diet Coke throughout. I'm here to help you make more positive financial decisions (if your idea of financial security involves spending most of your money on wine).

SOUTH AFRICAN CHENIN

The homeland of Chenin Blanc is the Loire Valley, but South Africa is the grape's second home. Cuttings came to South Africa during the time of the Cape Colony, and it is now the most widely planted grape in the country. While Loire expressions will err on the side of elegance, South African Chenin can be a little more robust, with notes of tropical fruits and more obvious use of oak. It's a wine that's commonly available at most indie bottle shops and supermarkets.

CAN'T FIND IT? TRY THIS:

If you're after something with a similar flavour profile, go for the opulence of a New World Chardonnay, one that's seen some time in oak, and that shows the same food-friendly generosity of tropical fruit, underpinned by a great acidity.

—

COLOUR:
white

NOTABLE REGIONS:
Swartland, Stellenbosch, Coastal Region, Paarl

ON THE LABEL:
it will nearly always say 'Chenin Blanc' on the label. South Africa will probably be stated there too, but keep an eye out for specific regions

A

NIGHT

OUT

PRE-DRINKS

Why is it that at the climax of the week, we all develop the thirst of a 17-year-old whose parents are away for the weekend? How does the mere mention of the F word kickstart a Gondor-like call to arms, concerned only with something long, cold and frosty? I'm not a fan of generalising nationalities, but this weirdly pathological urge is something I've noticed to be uniquely British. Another one of these things is pre-drinks. Within each Brit, we possess an innate need to drink to prepare for . . . more drinking. But I don't have space in this book to psychoanalyse that.

I'm not a big pre-drinker anymore. I work in wine, so my life is now essentially one big pre-drink preparing me for the grave. But if you possess the age or temperament whereby you can still pre-drink, you'll need something that's easily drunk, simple and fresh – something so unassuming and pleasant it absolves any sins in advance. After all, nothing bad has ever happened after one good glass of wine.

TGIF, to all who celebrate.

VINHO VERDE

On behalf of every sommelier and bottle shop owner: no, it isn't green. It's white, it's from Portugal, and it's the galvanising tincture you need for a night out. Brimming with energy, it's often inexpensive and a light effervescence makes it unabashedly quaffable. So, I'd buy it by the case, rather than by the bottle. You know how thirsty you get.

CAN'T FIND IT? TRY THIS:
Another wine that springs to mind when considering lively, exuberant whites is a Txakoli. Hailing from the Basque country in Spain, its vibrant character (and similar Vinho Verde spritz) makes it an equally appealing apéritif. You're more likely to find this in a speciality bottle shop – some of the supermarkets have a bit of catching up to do.

HENS/STAGS

There are occasions that you come across where the wine selection means nothing, and everything, all at once. Take hen and stag dos. The MO of the evening is not to sit quietly around a table, dutifully swirling, sniffing and saying things like, 'Oh yes, I'm really getting the wet stone in this one.'

If your idea of a successful hen-do necessitates a tedious wine circle-jerk, by all means, go ahead. I hope your marriage to that tax auditor works out. If you're feeling a little more pragmatic, then the wine for your bachelor party only really needs to do two things: it needs to be modest in ABV (you're in this for the long haul) and it needs to be delicious.

As much as I love wine – so much so that I decided to build a career around it – I don't believe it needs to always be the focal point of the evening. It's what I say to the attendees of my wine events. Sometimes we just need something inoffensive to move the evening along and let the important things in life take centre stage.

PROVENCE ROSÉ

Brimming with soft red fruit and with a precise mineral streak, Provence rosé is proper party fuel. Bone-dry and brimming with freshness, it's just what the doctor ordered. Actually, I don't think that's a real doctor. Why have they just taken their shirt off? And why are they sitting on the bride's face?

CAN'T FIND IT? TRY THIS:

If you're looking for something aesthetically similar, any other French rosé will do: seek out a Cabernet Franc rosé from the Loire if you can. And if your fragile masculinity is so insurmountable that you don't feel comfortable drinking something pink at a stag do, don't go too hard on the night, you've got your GCSEs to revise for in the morning.

—

COLOUR:
pink

NOTABLE GRAPES:
Grenache, Syrah, Mourvèdre, Cabernet Sauvignon, Carignan, Cinsault, Tibouren

ON THE LABEL:
it will most likely say 'Côtes de Provence', or 'Provence' on the label

LAST-MINUTE PLANS

The story goes like this. You receive a text inciting last-minute plans, just as you're about to slip into something more comfortable (big t-shirt with mysterious stain). You realise you'd actually quite like to go out, and that friends are (occasionally) more important than Amazon Prime. Or, perhaps your friend has just had a break up (see page 48) and an emergency night out is required. A bottle of wine has a life expectancy of 24 hours in your house, so you've nothing in your wine rack. And so, to the supermarket or bottle shop, hoping to grab something good in the five minutes you've left yourself.

Realistically, I know we must leave ample time to make this most crucial of decisions. I like to have a full-blown conversation with whoever's working at the bottle shop that day, to stroll up and down the aisles as the bottles wink in the light of passing car headlights, soaking in the arresting display of labels, appellations and wax seals. As is my right. But you're often already running late in these situations, and not everyone can be afforded such luxuries. I'm often on the receiving end of panicked texts from my friends: 'If I send you a photo of the shelf in front of me, will you tell me what I should get?'

When we want a bottle of wine for some last-minute plans, what we're really asking for is something that's inoffensive on the palate, crowd-pleasing and satisfies that holiest of ratios: price to ABV. Look, just because we're older, doesn't mean we have to be wiser. Some things never change.

RED RIOJA

When you're snared into a last-minute dinner party, it's comforting knowing that a good bottle of red Rioja can be found in nearly every artisanal bottle shop, off-licence and supermarket. It's also my opinion that supermarket Riojas are some of the best-value wines you can get. I love Rioja in the same way many love their favourite pair of socks: doggedly reliable and intensely warming.

CAN'T FIND IT? TRY THIS:

Red Rioja is predominantly made from Tempranillo, so for wines made from the same grape, look for wines labelled Ribera del Duero, as well as blends from Portugal, where it's known as Tinta Roriz. For other warming corner-shop favourites, look for Cabernet blends, Shiraz and Malbec. Obviously, for wines that are more likely to be palatable, take the extra time to go to your local bottle shop over the local offie.

—

COLOUR:
red

NOTABLE GRAPES:
Tempranillo, Garnacha, Mazuelo and Graciano

ON THE LABEL:
it will always say 'Rioja' on the label

DINNER PARTY
(YOU KNOW EVERYONE GOING)

The dinner party is the new millennial status symbol. The ultimate Insta moment and the only instance anyone in my generation will ever be within 10 metres of a devilled egg.

Eggs aside, devilled or otherwise, a bottle of wine is also a focal point of the dinner party. You need something that's worthy of taking centre stage, but don't buy a wine because it has a swearword on its ironically-designed bottle. It's worth reminding ourselves that most amazing producers don't employ a full-time graphic designer. And, on the other side of the coin, some crap producers do. How often have you and your friends ordered a beautiful bottle only to take a sip, pull a face, and decide to promptly delete all of your Instagram stories? Be honest.

You need a wine of substance. You need a wine that tells a story, that sparks conversation and the imagination. In doing this, you'll mark yourself as the evening's wine expert, but please note page 102, dedicated to dinner parties where everyone there *is* a wine expert. That's a whole different ball game.

—

COLOUR:
white

NOTABLE
GRAPES:
Sauvignon Blanc

ON THE LABEL:
it will always say
'Pouilly-Fumé' on
the label

POUILLY-FUMÉ

In my experience, you can't go wrong with a
Pouilly-Fumé. It's made purely from
Sauvignon Blanc (often a total crowd-pleaser)
and comes from the Loire. A smoky, gun-flint
aroma sets it apart from the typical New
Zealand Sauvy B, a delicious way to branch
out from the tried-and-tested favourites. It also
goes nicely with eggs, incidentally.

CAN'T FIND IT? TRY THIS:

If you're dead-set on Sauvignon Blanc from
the Loire, look out for names from other
communes in the region: Sancerre and
Menetou-Salon are probably going to be your
best bet. For some more classic crowd-pleasers,
look for Pinot Noir, Côtes du Rhône or white
Burgundy.

DINNER PARTY
(YOU DON'T KNOW
ANYONE THERE)

Before any words are exchanged, any stories told, a bottle of wine conveys something about yourself to others. Nowhere is this more crucial than a dinner party where no one knows who you are. You're yet to make an impression, and wine helps you do just that.

To solve this problem in the past, you may well have turned to articles about 'dinner party wines'. They gleam with the promise of having found the wine for your evening plans. They also often possess a totally unchecked use of the word 'perfect'. For example: 15 sumptuous reds that are *perfect* for the colder months; nine rosés that pair *perfectly* with any side salad; 37 Pinot Grigios set to change the course of humanity and solve world hunger. You know, those ones.

These articles vow to strip decision paralysis from the wine aisle like hot wax. The wines are, after all, perfect. They do not, however, tell you what you actually need to know. Which is that no one at the party really cares that the wine you brought pairs well with the side salad. People are drinking differently now; it's why this book exists, and why you've turned to this page in last-minute panic.

All you actually need in order to save your bottle from relegation to the back of a cupboard is a good story. Perhaps the wine was a happy accident born of a misguided cellar experiment; perhaps the wine style is unexpected for the region; perhaps you met the winemaker at a fair and they mistakenly flirted with your partner.

You need two sentences, tops. People love a good tidbit, something to pique the interest. To bastardise an important quote from Maya Angelou: 'People will forget about the soggy side salad, people will forget the host's annoying dog, but people will never forget how your wine made them feel.'

WHITE BORDEAUX

Yes, another Sauvignon Blanc for a dinner party. Yes, they do white wine in Bordeaux. Made from Sauvignon Blanc – although most blends include a dash of Sémillon and/or Muscadelle – its fresh, creamy notes of lemon curd and gooseberry are sure to appeal to the Sauvignon Blanc devotees. 'I didn't know they did white Bordeaux!' is what they'll say. Conversation flows freely (as does the wine), your place in the social group secured by a single bottle of the good stuff – perfect.

CAN'T FIND IT? TRY THIS:

Opt for a Sancerre (from the Loire), Adelaide Hills (from Australia) or a Chilean wine (some fabulous wines can be found in Aconcagua).

—

COLOUR:
white

NOTABLE GRAPES:
Sauvignon Blanc, Sémillon, Muscadelle

ON THE LABEL:
unless the bottle is marked 'Bordeaux Superieur', it's unlikely you'll see the word 'Bordeaux' on the label. Instead, keep an eye out for names of châteaux and appellations (see page 24)

DINNER PARTY (EVERYONE THERE IS A 'WINE PERSON')

I love going to dinner parties with wine people. It's like walking into a room where everyone also had an anime phase as a child or where everyone grew up in the same obscure part of the country as you. There's also no pressure to be the 'wine friend', as everyone equally shares the burden of being the most oenologically literate. I am understood. I am at home.

But for those of you not within the secret circle, the prospect of this situation could not be more toe-curling. It's the lion's den. The pit of vipers. A version of the recurring dream you have where everyone is clothed at the dinner table except you, and all you have to cover your modesty is a bottle of Casillero del Diablo. You wake up sweating and breathless. What on earth should you bring?

Winos are complex but simple creatures. We love bottles with fuck-off price tags as much as we adore value (we are notoriously underpaid). We love the thrill of an unexpected bottle as much as we love the classics with a château on the label. I know it's easy for me to say, but my best piece of advice would be to not overthink it. Just like any dinner party you're likely to go to, everyone in attendance will have a different palate, different likes and a different idea of what it is that will go best with the meal itself.

What I'm trying to say is, not everyone will like the wine you bring, and that's OK. Instead, I'm going to offer three wine options that I'd bring to please the palates of my wine friends. They go down well among most, a good combination of what I like to call thinking wines and drinking wines. Thinking wines being the bottle you dutifully swill and sniff while you ponder things like lees-ageing and terroir. Drinking wines are the ones that have you dancing on tables and pouring wine from great heights, ruining the Rick Owens you rented from a financial consultant in Canada Water, plus any modest chance you may have had of getting off with that hot somm. Better luck next time. With these three bottles, there definitely will be a next time.

MEURSAULT

In the much-hailed wine film *Sour Grapes*, Burgundy is described as the choice region for wine nerds. As generalisations go about winos, this one certainly holds water. Burgundy is so broad in the styles it can yield, there's something there for everybody. But Meursault, I've noticed, holds a special place in the hearts of somms and industry-types alike. Usually 100% Chardonnay, Meursault is one of the more seductive, hedonistic examples of white Burgundy. Honeyed, nutty, creamy, this is a proper push-the-boat-out bottle that no wine person with a functioning palate could turn down.

CAN'T FIND IT? TRY THIS:
This is where you can pretend to flex your wine knowledge a bit. Meursault is probably the most commonly known fancy white Burgundy from the Côte de Beune, so choosing similarly styled wines from neighbouring appellations Puligny-Montrachet or Chassagne-Montrachet will earn you extra brownie points.

—

COLOUR:
white

NOTABLE GRAPES:
Chardonnay

ON THE LABEL:
a Meursault wine will always state its name on the label

XINOMAVRO

At the time of writing, Greek wines are beginning to 'have a moment'. Slowly, lesser-known varieties are sneaking onto wine lists and shop shelves. Xinomavro is a popular native red grape variety that makes bright, yet structured wines, with notes of fresh red fruits, olives and dried herbs. Think of it like a Greek Nebbiolo (the grape used to make Barolo and Barbaresco).

—

COLOUR:
red

NOTABLE REGIONS:
Greece

ON THE LABEL:
it will nearly always say 'Xinomavro' on the label

CAN'T FIND IT? TRY THIS:
While Xinomavro is one of the most popular Greek grape varieties, there are loads that are available to whet your appetite. For a crisp, saline white, try Assyrtiko. For something aromatic and peachy, seek out Moschofilero.

FINO SHERRY

Yes, you read that right. When I was a kid, there was a fabulously funny book where an elderly woman was seemingly always drinking sherry that she hid in her walking stick. That stereotype prevails: that you need to be from a certain generation to enjoy it. Another stereotype that prevails is that all sherry is sticky and tastes of raisins, when the region actually produces a range of delicious styles. A lip-smacking wine to kick off an evening would be a bottle of Fino, one of the lightest styles of sherry. It's sharp, energising and has a moreish umami taste of salted almonds.

COLOUR:
white

NOTABLE GRAPES:
Palomino, Pedro Ximénez

ON THE LABEL:
it will always say 'Fino' on the label

CAN'T FIND IT? TRY THIS:

Another lighter style of sherry is Manzanilla, which is made in the same way as Fino sherry but can only be made in the coastal town of Sanlúcar de Barrameda. Because it's made close to the sea, Manzanilla sherry tends to be a bit more saline, with less of that obvious savoury character that Fino has. Perhaps this is the bottle to select if you're a first-time sherry drinker.

YOU'RE IN A LIMOUSINE
(FOR SOME REASON)

There are many reasons why you could be in a limo, all of them deeply sordid. Unless you're literally the dude on the Monopoly box, you're unlikely to be spending your entire evening in a limo. A limo is a way to get from A to B (if A stands for 'a drink' and B stands for 'booze'). It's a means to a messy end. It is proms, hens, stags and cringeworthy corporate events. It is all four horsemen of the requisite social situation apocalypse.

Unless there is a built-in Champagne bottle and glasses that emerge from between the seats like buried treasure (I hope your date with James Bond goes well), you'll need to acquire sufficient libation before revving up to 20mph down the M40. A wine that's fit to be consumed on the go, whether you're facing the front, sitting sideways or facing backwards, trying to win a battle against your acid reflux. I find something with bubbles settles the stomach (when I'm hungover, I fantasise about a can of ginger beer emerging from a lake in a white shirt, Darcy style), plus, sparkling wines inject a little fun into the most soporific of situations. Fill her up, Tina, and tell me more about your new gravel driveway.

ROSÉ PROSECCO

It's fruit forward, but not too sweet, and now, thanks to new legislation, the quality of pink Prosecco has soared. It's made by a different method to crémant: the second fermentation takes place in a large tank rather than a bottle, a method that increases the intensity of the 'mousse', which means more bubbles, and more pink. This is high camp in a wine.

CAN'T FIND IT? TRY THIS:
Méthode Cap Classique (often abbreviated to MCC) is also available in pink. This is a similarly affordable wine produced in South Africa, using the exact same winemaking process as Champagne. Or, if you're hankering after something Italian, sparkling and camp, a frothy Lambrusco will fit the bill.

—

COLOUR:
pink (sparkling)

NOTABLE GRAPES:
predominantly Glera, blended with 10–15% of Pinot Noir

ON THE LABEL:
Pink Prosecco became legally official in 2020 and government-approved bottles state 'Prosecco DOC Rosé' on the label

MEETING UP WITH OLD FRIENDS

They say the only two things certain in life are death and taxes, but I'd like to propose a third thing: change. Change is an inevitability, which, at times, can feel electrifying and life-affirming. It feels like things are *moving forward*. But constant change can also feel relentless, even if you manage to get life exactly how you like it, even if you so desperately want everything to stay the same.

That is why, in my opinion, it is especially important (/impressive) to maintain relationships with old friends. These people are your constant, somewhere between a parent (offering sage advice) and a sibling (winding you up and stealing your clothes). These are relationships of a life-altering quality, which means, naturally, you see them every six years.

Now, this is definitely an occasion to make an effort, as is your right – how often do you get to do this? But, at the same time, these are easy people to impress. They're not the cool couple you met on a cruise you're desperate to be real-life friends with; they're not your in-laws (see page 38) or someone you're trying to shag. These are real friends, and real friends don't really care what you bring. 'Just bring yourself' is the age-old adage, but wouldn't it be better if you arrived with a bottle of something remarkable?

AUSTRALIAN RIESLING

One of my close friends in the industry, Freddy Bulmer, is a buyer for Australia, and is of the opinion that its Rieslings are some of the most underrated in the world. And it's true. As the prices of revered European Rieslings rise, Rieslings from the Clare and Eden Valleys are gaining a mainstream reputation for just how brilliant, and what great value, they are. This way, you can get something special, without anyone feeling like they need to transfer you £5. They're bone-dry, floral and brimming with citrus and stone fruit.

COLOUR:
white

NOTABLE REGIONS:
Clare Valley, Eden Valley

ON THE LABEL:
New World Riesling will nearly always say 'Riesling' on the label

CAN'T FIND IT? TRY THIS:

For other wines that punch well above their price point, try Aligoté from Burgundy (nowhere near as expensive as white Burgundy but just as invigorating), Xinomavro from Greece (like a cross between Nebbiolo and Pinot Noir), Verdicchio from Italy (great for lovers of Loire Sauvignon Blanc) or Valpolicella (ridiculously underpriced considering the amount of time that goes into this plush wine, but more on that on page 150).

PERSONAL

DRINKING

WHEN YOU DON'T WANT TO DRINK WINE

'Hi Hannah, do you have any recommendations on what I should drink if I don't really feel like drinking wine?' I remember the first time I got this message. My knee-jerk reaction: 'Girl, just don't drink wine lol,' but then I remembered all the times that I've felt the same.

Sometimes, you want to pile onto the sofa with an oven pizza and a glass of something distinctly un-wine-like. Sometimes, for no discernible reason, wine is just giving you . . . the ick?

At certain times of the year, or the month, the very thought of a glass of wine makes me feel ill. Wine appears to me (mostly when I'm hungover) as a syrupy, tannic, nauseating brew. Sometimes you just can't be arsed with the heavy stuff. And that's OK. What's needed is something simple, something fresh, something so intensely satisfying that only a single glass will do, and I have just the thing.

LAMBRUSCO

The delight that Lambrusco brings is usually only reserved for children's books. There's something very Tove Jansson about the joyful mulberry colour, the fluffy pink foam. It's 'Why the hell not?' in a glass. There are many variations in sweetness, colour and varietal blend, but the style of Lambrusco I want to drink is a brilliant deep purple, bone-dry with a gentle sparkle. It's often got a low ABV and, for me at least, one glass is more than enough.

CAN'T FIND IT? TRY THIS:
For a similar frothy exuberance, I'd opt for a pét-nat. Made using the ancestral method, it's more of a delicate fizz than a downright sparkle. It comes in every colour too, so if you're feeling more like a pink than a red, there'll be something to tickle your fancy.

—

COLOUR:
red

NOTABLE REGIONS:
Emilia-Romagna

NOTABLE GRAPES:
Lambrusco Grasparossa, Lambrusco Maestri, Lambrusco Marani, Lambrusco Montericco, Lambrusco Salamino and Lambrusco Sorbara are the most common Lambrusco varieties

ON THE LABEL:
it will always say 'Lambrusco' on the label

YOU'VE JUST HAD A BABY

As far as I can tell, giving birth seems a lot like when I used to go out raving. Ten to twenty hours of restless movement, then, back to yours with achy joints and a person in tow you've never met. Then, experiencing a lot of pain and discomfort, you don't really leave the house for a considerable time after. Except, it's not a sleep paralysis demon staring at you from an unwashed pile of clothes at the other end of the room, it's a human life that entirely depends on you for its survival.

Understandably, you don't feel a lot like drinking (I'm obviously referring to the birth-giver in this scenario, with little in the way of sympathy for the partner who's been necking pints since the first trimester). But you've been through such a dry patch to get here, you feel as though you *should*. Each of your life's achievements has been punctuated with a glass of something, if not a full-blown night out.

You've also signed up to a new, second, unpaid career as a human–cow hybrid. But you're not allowed to drink on the job. This is the reason you won't see many new mothers taking postpartum tequila shots, or a glass of wine, on the sofa. However, it's totally safe for new mums to have a single drink a couple of hours before they plan to breastfeed, or directly after. People I know have said that a single glass of wine at the end of the day is an important moment of me-time they look forward to. So, if you're a friend of a new mother, a bottle of wine will most definitely be a welcome gift.

OFF-DRY RIESLING

Some real thought has gone into this one, and after much sampling and asking several new mums I know, I've come to the conclusion that an off-dry Riesling is the best port of call. It needs to be a still wine so that it keeps well in the fridge and you're able to enjoy a single glass each day over a longer period of time. It's often low in alcohol (a personal supermarket favourite is only 8%), and is delightfully sweet, with notes of lemon, peach and honey from the late-harvest grapes. Look for wines labelled Spätlese and Auslese.

CAN'T FIND IT? TRY THIS:

The key thing here is a wine that will keep. For this reason, high-quality boxed wines are also a brilliant port of call. They're not just astringent Merlot and grassy Sauvignon anymore. Plus, some of the best examples will keep for up to six weeks after opening.

—

COLOUR:
white

NOTABLE REGIONS:
Mosel, Rheingau, Hungary, Austria, New Zealand, United States, Canada

ON THE LABEL:
the word 'Riesling' is unlikely to feature on a German bottle. Instead, keep an eye out for the elongated bottle shape and the different Riesling sweetness designations: Kabinett, Spätlese, Auslese, Beerenauslese, Trockenbeerenauslese and Eiswein

YOU'RE A SMOKER

I laid down the bulk of this book smoking heavily at my desk and, while I'm not advocating for anyone to take up smoking, the fact is we're still out there, decreasing in number though we are. Like most smokers, I utilise the act to inject a little 'me-time' into the day, in the same way other (healthier) people use a 43-step skincare routine or mindfulness journalling. My desk looks out onto a beautiful green park in East London, where an inexcusably gorgeous runner dashes past every few seconds. I look down from my ivory tower, tutting.

Smoking can ease the tedium of the 9 to 5. It's a habit I first picked at 17 (sorry mum) to escape a particularly cruel chef three times a day for five succulent minutes (I even started smoking super kings so I could bump it up to ten). I'm a freelancer now, but the habit has stuck and I can't get rid, like a lovely but needlessly chatty person sat next to you on a plane.

Being a smoker working in wine brings up an inevitable line of questioning, each inquiry more tedious than the last. The most impertinent, however, is the question on whether it affects taste. It doesn't inhibit your drinking experience, so how should it mine? The wine industry has no shortage of smokers. I just got back from a trip to France where most *vigneron* punctuated each sentence with a hand-rolled cigarette. As is their god-given right.

PINOT NOIR

This is a wine match made in heaven. Pinot Noir is likely to be on by the glass at whatever Parisian bistro or Mancunian pub garden you're likely to find. It's light enough for the experience to not overpower, and I find something overly tannic makes a cigarette taste a little too dry (a bulky Claret is more cigar territory, right?). A simple glass of Pinot will do nicely. Leave the bottle though, thanks.

CAN'T FIND IT? TRY THIS:

Other smoky wines include the wines of northern Italy (Barolo, Barbaresco), Pinotage, Carménère and many red wines from the Southern Rhône. If white wine is more your style, you'll find that Pouilly-Fumé has a delicious gunflint smoke (hence the 'fumé').

COLOUR:
red

NOTABLE REGIONS:
Burgundy, Champagne, California, New Zealand, Australia, Chile, England

ON THE LABEL:
'New World' countries will nearly always say 'Pinot Noir' on the label. Most wines from Burgundy will only state the appellation or cru (head to page 24 to see if the name on the bottle is an appellation)

A FIRST-EVER BOTTLE OF WINE

I remember my first bottle of wine. It was a little later than most – 16 is prehistoric in British terms – but for good reason. You may not be able to conceive of it, and for that I will forgive you, but I didn't grow up with many friends. As such, opportunities to participate in illegal teenage drinking were few and far between. And, to add insult to injury, I simply wasn't allowed to drink at parties. To provide crucial context, my mum is a social worker specialising in children's protection, so you can slightly understand her desire to not have one of her own wrapped around a tree pumped full of Apple Sourz.

However, at one particular function, in a controlled environment where for every child there were about seven adults, she allowed me to have a drink of my choice. I selected a bottle of rosé from a brand I won't name drop, just know that it rhymes with Gecko Balls. I travelled to the party clutching hold of it, allowing the rosé to warm nicely on my lap, excited to take my first sip of adulthood.

I arrived at the party, under the watchful eye of my parents, and poured myself a glass. Unsurprisingly, I hated it. Looking back with the halcyon hindsight gleaned from a thousand tastings, it was sugary and poorly balanced. At the time, I just thought I hated wine. Tears in my eyes, I reached for a Coke Zero instead. The fizzy triage.

I wish that my first wine experience had been one that kicked off my career a few years earlier. I'm here to ensure that your first bottle of wine offers excitement and curiosity. Who knows, you could be a Master of Wine before you hit thirty – anything is possible.

BLAUFRÄNKISCH

Simply made, fruity wines are an excellent place to kick off a lifelong obsession. Indeed, this was the avenue many took to learning about wine during lockdown. And while there are plenty of deliciously complex, layered presentations of Blaufränkisch (I have plenty of them in my wine cupboard), sometimes a simple, juicy Blau is what's needed. This is a wine made across central Europe, so expect to see Austria or the Czech Republic on the bottle. I can't think of a more joyful introduction to the world of wine.

—

COLOUR:
red

NOTABLE REGIONS:
Austria, Czech Republic, Germany, Slovakia

ON THE LABEL:
100% Blaufränkisch wines will nearly always say 'Blaufränkisch' on the label

CAN'T FIND IT? TRY THIS:
Fruit-forward wines are the way to go, but will really vary from vendor to vendor. To be sure you're getting a well-made wine that's also approachable, I recommend going to your local bottle shop for this over the supermarket. Ask the owner what they'd recommend for a first-timer – you'll walk out with something tasty.

YOU JUST QUIT YOUR JOB

White vests, hot sauce, turning left. There are a lot of things we must credit Beyoncé with popularising, but I think the one thing that most of us are thankful for is the part 'BREAK MY SOUL' had to play in the mass resignation of 2022.

The song was inescapable that summer, when a record number of workers emancipated themselves from their jobs post-COVID. Bey's powerful vocals put forth a rallying cry to quit your job and find a new drive (although exactly what job she's considering quitting, I'm not so sure).

The past few years have seen a real shift in power from the employer to the worker – the Oompa Loompa has shares in Wonka Bars. Quitting a job you hate isn't the black mark on your CV that it used to be and a long gap is no longer automatically attributed to joining a cult. This generation has a life of jobs, not a job for life, and the brief stint between each is a miraculous opportunity to refocus. Take a breath. Move forward. Pour yourself a drink.

—

COLOUR:
pink (sparkling)

NOTABLE
GRAPES:
Chardonnay, Pinot
Noir, Chenin Blanc,
Cabernet Franc,
Grolleau and many
others, depending
on the region

ON THE LABEL:
it will always say
'Crémant' on the
label

CRÉMANT ROSÉ

It's pink and has bubbles in it – this is classy
celebration at its best. The bottle of Crémant –
whether it be from the Loire, Burgundy,
Alsace or anywhere else – is a cost-effective
way to celebrate. And, let's be honest, you
might need to pinch those pennies until you
find your feet again. But hey, just because it's
not Champers, doesn't mean it's not delicious.

CAN'T FIND IT? TRY THIS:
Rosé Prosecco is made by a different method
to Crémant: the second fermentation takes
place in a large tank rather than a bottle. Since
the Italian government approved the
production of rosé Prosecco, quality has only
improved.

YOU WANT TO PRETEND YOU KNOW A LOT ABOUT WINE

When you're first getting into wine, there's a certain degree to which you have to fake it till you make it. It's like starting a job that you're underqualified for or dating people who are significantly hotter than you. Most of wine is about knowledge, but until you garner that knowledge, a great deal of it is about having confidence. This is probably the reason I started my career online, as many do.

I'll be the first to profess I don't know everything about wine. Which is true for nearly all wine professionals, no one *can* know everything. I take a fair bit of comfort, knowing that everyone, whether they've been in the industry for 20 years or 20 minutes, is always learning. There will always be a new producer, a new vintage, a new innovation.

So, if you're planning on ordering from a list or bringing a bottle to an event that makes you look like you know a lot, don't overthink it. I know people with WSET Diplomas that bring cheap (but excruciatingly delicious) Verdicchio to wine dinners. There are also those who will go out of their way (and into their overdraft) bringing the most ego-extending limited-edition cuvée from a little-known-winery-that-you-probably-haven't-heard-of-anyway-and-even-if-you-did-their-entire-vineyard-burnt-to-the-ground-last-year. Don't be like these people. Be more like you, but with a touch of wine-stained confidence in your step. Eliza Doolittle has become the Hungarian princess. The student has become the master. Sparkling grape juice has become liquid confidence.

ENGLISH SPARKLING WINE

Pull up to the average function with a bottle of English sparkling, and you'll be met with two reactions. Firstly, an earnest, 'I didn't know they made wine in England?' In this person's eyes, you're already a genius. The second type of person you'll meet will say, 'I knew they did English sparkling wine, but I heard it wasn't any good.' Bring along a bottle of quality English Blanc de Noirs (sparkling wine made from 100% Pinot Noir) and you'll show them not only is English sparkling wine incredible, but that you really know your stuff.

CAN'T FIND IT? TRY THIS:

For wines that are sure to impress, see page 102, dedicated to what to bring to a dinner party to impress wine people.

—

COLOUR:
white

NOTABLE GRAPES:
Chardonnay, Pinot Noir, Pinot Meunier (the Champagne ones)

ON THE LABEL:
some English sparkling wines will say so on the label, some will just have the name of the winery and some will also mention the location of the vineyard e.g. Sussex, Dorset or Hampshire

SOMEONE ELSE IS PAYING

I often say something pretentious and saccharine about language being the biggest barrier facing people who want to get into wine. That's just faux intellectualism. In this life, there is no bigger barrier than money.

Have you ever heard the phrase 'Champagne drinker on a Prosecco budget'? That's the reality of working in wine, where a full day's work on the floor *might* afford you the list price of a bottle of the wine you've been pouring all night. I'm a freelance wine writer, which means I'm more than likely to be caught red-handed with a bottle of Côtes du Rhône or Bourgogne Blanc. I'm sure if I had more money I'd be a much more sophisticated drinker, using my cavernous wallet to explore the grands crus and niche appellations with abandon, on a keen mission to develop gout before the age of 30. But alas, there's a reason I'm always waxing lyrical about finding value in wine. It's not just for your benefit.

So, what do you buy when money is no object? Perhaps you're getting treated to a nice meal, it's your birthday or you're out for a date with someone who gets a kick from spaffing lots of money. But what if you're not one of those people who'll enter a restaurant with the full confidence to ask the somm to bring their finest bottle? How do you have any frame of reference of what to order when that time comes? It's somehow more daunting than ordering a wine with no money.

BRUNELLO DI MONTALCINO

—

Oh, any bottle, you say? Milk the opportunity. I, personally, would opt for a Brunello di Montalcino. If you're at a serious restaurant (which I assume you are, if you're so panicked that you've pulled out a book in advance), they're bound to have one on the menu. This is a wine from Tuscany, made from Sangiovese, which is also the main component for Chianti and many Super Tuscan blends. This is an incredibly lavish wine that must undergo five years ageing before it's legally allowed to be released. The result: rich, indulgent notes of espresso, dried berries and liquorice. It's pretty tannic though, so best to order this one with some food.

COLOUR:
red

NOTABLE GRAPES:
Sangiovese

ON THE LABEL:
it will always say 'Brunello di Montalcino' on the label

CAN'T FIND IT? TRY THIS:
Picking one fancy wine for this page was nigh on impossible, as nearly every winemaking region has its own standout wine that you'd be daft to not pick on a wine list. Mature Chablis. Anything from a sainted Napa winery. Blood-red Barolo. Red or white Burgundy from a cru I haven't explored yet. The same for the Rhône. New Zealand Pinot Noir that pirouettes on the tongue. Most things Spanish. Impossibly perfumed German Riesling. Champagne.

YOU'RE WATCHING TV

Sometimes, a good Friday night doesn't involve a cave à vin and dropping £60 on a skilfully made wine, even for a devotee. Sometimes you don't need to venture far from home to enjoy a good glass of wine.

Most wine, where I grew up anyway, is consumed curled up like a bratwurst on the sofa, sizzling or seething at the latest post-apocalyptic reality TV you're ashamed to adore.

At home, wine is consumed a glass at a time. It sits in the door of your fridge or quietly slumbering on a wine rack, occasionally dipped into like an overdraft the last week before payday. Whatever's on, I love a glass of something to fuel my over-involvement in other peoples' lives. So, with this in mind, I'm not going to suggest something you need to finish in a day once it's opened. Something you can enjoy over the next days, weeks, even up to a month.

RUBY PORT

'Hannah, I thought this book was for what you keep obnoxiously trying to coin "a new wave of wine drinkers", not my grandfather watching reruns of *Only Fools and Horses* at Christmas. I'm watching the TV, not lying comatose in front of it.' I get it, port and its ruddy-cheeked devotees are very easy to stereotype as a bit pale, stale and male. The patriarchal triple threat. But port is so bloody

delicious it's well deserving of a modern renaissance. There are many different types of port, but Ruby port, which I'm suggesting here, has more of a spring in its step than other styles. It's younger, fruity, and it can last for more than a month in the fridge after it's been opened. But I doubt you'll need more than a week to polish it off.

CAN'T FIND IT? TRY THIS:
Tawny port tends to be aged for a similar length of time to Ruby port (between one and three years). However, just as with many other wines, there are quality levels. Look for the word 'Reserve' on the label, which denotes a Ruby or Tawny port that's been determined as a high quality by an expert tasting panel. Definitely one to crack open for the *Love Island* final.

—

COLOUR:
red

NOTABLE GRAPES:
Tinta Barroca, Tinto Cão, Tinta Roriz, Touriga Francesa and Touriga Nacional are the most commonly used varieties, although over 100 are permitted for port production

ON THE LABEL:
it will always say 'Ruby Port' on the label

YOU'VE JUST WORKED OUT

Many people have a complicated relationship with exercise, and I am one of them. Exercise is a man I've been falling out of love with since my first PE lesson and has never been a part of my daily routine. This has only got worse since I started working in wine.

This is something many of my friends who work in food and drink experience. How can you indulge in everything you want to without your liver, gut and brain paying the price (in that order)? How can you have your cake and eat it? Your wine and drink it?

In a bid to be healthier (whilst not complaining so much that the wine stops flowing), a lot of us engage in a bit of tit for tat. They'll try to get in 10,000 steps because they went out for that extravagant meal last night. They'll work out because they got in at 4am. I'm the type to beg for forgiveness rather than ask for permission.

So, perhaps you're heading to a bar post hitting the gym after work, or maybe you're heading straight home for a glass of something enlivening. If you're the type to work out in the morning, the same rules apply – no judgement.

CALIFORNIAN CHARDONNAY

I don't know about you, but I crave something fructose and sweet after working out. Something to get the blood sugar back up. One of the best things about Chardonnay is that it possesses a playdough-like pliability, with an ability to express its terroir and climate with perfect elocution. Californian Chardonnay tends to be big, fruity and buttery, but with a good acidity to keep the big flavours in check. I need a good balance of sugar and acidity to keep me refreshed (note how it's the same grape variety I advise for post-coital refreshment on page 44). Keep a bottle in your fridge for when you get back from your afternoon run.

CAN'T FIND IT? TRY THIS:
Put the reds away for this one. For the same reasons stated above, I love a New World Riesling. One from Australia (in particular the Clare Valley and Eden Valley regions) will do the trick. Or perhaps an off-dry German Riesling. If you can hack something a bit more aromatic, go for a Sauvignon Blanc.

—

COLOUR:
white

NOTABLE GRAPES:
Chardonnay

ON THE LABEL:
it will nearly always say 'Chardonnay' on the label

YOU'RE HUNGOVER

What's your favourite part of George Orwell's *Animal Farm*? Mine is when the pigs get a hangover.

Forget the mordant political satire of this timeless novella, this is the scene that sticks with me. In Chapter 8, tyrannical porcine douchebag Napoleon discovers a case of whisky in the farmhouse, which later results in an awful lot of loud singing and dancing in the back garden in a bowler hat. The next morning, the animals are solemnly gathered and told that Comrade Napoleon is dying, pronouncing as his last act upon earth that the consumption of alcohol is to be punishable by death. By the next day, he's fine, so much so that he instructs one of the other pigs to purchase some booklets on brewing and distilling, presumably to open an urban brewery under a railway arch in East London.

We've all been there. Napoleon's near-death experience has a little of all of us within it. The renouncing of alcohol, so convinced of the singularity of your experience (no one else has ever been this hungover, surely?), only to learn nothing. I've died this way many times, but as many of you reading this will know, there isn't necessarily enough time to shake off the effects of last night before you're honour-bound to move onto the next.

Urban remedies and hastily ordered takeaways aside, I'm one to administer a little hair of the dog in such situations. Because, if drinking this evening is inevitable and impending, it's good to get back on the horse rather than get trampled by it.

MOSCATO D'ASTI

This is a good thing to have in the fridge.
Moscato d'Asti is a DOCG sparkling white
from northwestern Italy. Moscato was
traditionally a wine that winemakers made for
themselves to drink at lunchtime, but it's gone
through something of a modern renaissance
too, popularised thanks to Drake's verse on
the hilariously named song 'I Invented Sex'
('It's a celebration clap clap bravo / Lobster
and shrimp and a glass of Moscato'). It's
deliciously sweet and low in alcohol, just the
thing to bring you back from the brink of
death and on track for a good night out.

CAN'T FIND IT? TRY THIS:
A pét-nat is also a brilliant first drink to have
on a hangover. Lightly sparkling, low in ABV
and so fruity it may as well be a can of
Rubicon. If you can't stomach bubbles, opt for
a Riesling with some residual sweetness to get
your blood sugar levels up. Normal service has
resumed. See you on the dance floor, brave
soldier.

—

COLOUR:
white (sparkling)

NOTABLE
GRAPES:
Moscato Bianco

ON THE LABEL:
it will always say
'Moscato d'Asti' on
the label

YOU'RE ON YOUR PERIOD

Being an irreverent female writer who lives in East London, I am contractually obliged to spend at least two pages talking about periods. All I can say is that I'm glad for the rise of streaming services because it means I may never have to watch another advert for sanitary products – the ones that claim all that's holding any of us back from presenting an Apple keynote in space is the correct girth of tampon. I know I don't speak for everyone, but this is not my experience.

Every person who has a period has their own personal brand of excruciating hell that is unique and beautiful and special to them. The painters are in, and they've done a messy job on the skirting boards.

For myself, and many others, periods involve a great deal of crying and swearing, brought on by a unique hormonal frustration that nothing feels *right*. We don't feel right, our clothes don't fit right, our partners aren't speaking to us right and now, as it is my sad duty to inform you as you reach for that glass of wine, it probably won't *taste* right, either.

Yes, even your tastes change during your period. But that's not all, it also depends on *where* you are in your cycle. A recent study has found that in the first two weeks, oestrogen rises, increasing your sensitivity to flavour, so you'll tend to favour softer flavour profiles. Then, as oestrogen drops and progesterone rises, foods seem blander, so bolder flavours are critical in weeks three and four to satisfy us. No matter what season it is in your own special ring of hell, a big glass of liquid sanity is exactly what's needed. No notes from me.

WEEKS ONE AND TWO
SOAVE

I love a glass of Soave at any time of the month. It seems to be a wine that's readily available from most supermarkets, but I rarely hear it talked about by everyday drinkers. In the wine world, however, it is revered as a failsafe, uplifting glass of white, with notes of citrus, melon and a touch of salinity. The bright flavours of a youthful Soave will bring some much-needed freshness to the palate in the first two weeks of your cycle.

CAN'T FIND IT? TRY THIS:

In terms of other wines, Pinot Grigio, Pecorino and Fiano are good options. Be sure to look for youthful, unoaked expressions if you're searching for something gentle, as powerful, full-bodied versions of these wines definitely exist. Try a Riesling marked 'Kabinett' (the driest classification for Riesling) or a Vinho Verde.

—

COLOUR:
white

NOTABLE REGIONS:
Veneto, Italy

NOTABLE GRAPES:
Garganega, although some Trebbiano di Soave and Chardonnay is permitted

ON THE LABEL:
it will always say 'Soave' on the label

WEEKS THREE AND FOUR
ZINFANDEL

Zinfandel is a name you might be familiar with: an unapologetically bold, fruity red that satisfies a pre-menstrual craving for sweet jamminess. It's the fourth most-planted grape in California, but it's found a second home in the UK's mainstream drinking, meaning it's going to be easily picked up if you get a sudden craving on the commute. There's a bit of snobbery in the wine world about Zinfandel, but if bold, luscious wines are your thing, who am I to argue with you? No, seriously, an argument with a pre-menstrual person? Nice try.

CAN'T FIND IT? TRY THIS:

Try searching for Primitivo: this is a grape that's genetically identical to Zinfandel. Its heartland is Puglia, where you mostly see it varietally labelled as 'Primitivo', where it produces similarly bold wines, with notes of jammy berry fruit, spice and herbs.

—

COLOUR:
red

NOTABLE REGIONS:
California, Puglia, Croatia

ON THE LABEL:
'New World' countries will nearly always say 'Zinfandel' on the label

YOU'VE JUST ORDERED
A MASSIVE TAKEAWAY

I've gone to great lengths to explain that this is not a food and wine pairing book (for some brilliant books that do this exact thing, and do it well, look for my recommendations on page 12). *However*, it would be completely remiss of me, in a book that seeks to document life's great moments with bottles of wine, to redact the life-altering power of a good takeaway.

I've always been drawn to the highbrow/lowbrow moments that wine can enable. Grosses Gewächs Riesling with Monster Munch. Off-dry rosé with a lamb bhuna. Have you ever seen the film *Sideways*? Miles' 1961 Cheval Blanc is referenced throughout, a legendary Bordeaux from one of the most noteworthy vintages of the twentieth century. He knows that the bottle is about to peak and begin its slow decline, but is resistant to opening it, seemingly waiting until the perfect moment to do so. But, as in many other instances in this film, Miles' reluctance to carpe those diems means he misses out on many mundane, but important, moments that could change his life for the better. Realising this at the end of the film, he embraces life's absurdity, enjoying his Cheval Blanc from a polystyrene cup with a burger in a fast-food restaurant.

Although our lives are occasionally afforded these so-called perfect moments, the type Miles hopes for throughout the film, the rest of our time on this earth is laced with tedium and mundanity. We can't ignore these in pursuit of times that may never come. Before we know it, it will all be over and there will be no more wine. And then, what will we do?

Don't wait until Christmas or New Year's Eve to open a special bottle (although you should definitely turn to pages 174 and 180 if you plan on doing so anyway). Celebrate the everyday just as opulently. And what's more ordinary, more delicious, more commonplace, more intimate and more personal than a hastily ordered, oily, far too big takeaway?

VIOGNIER

—

If you do have the chance to prepare for your dine-in banquet, go for Viognier. Viognier, a grape variety originating from southern France, yields several styles. What unites them all, however, is an intense, perfumed bouquet of peach, white flowers, vanilla, rose and tangerine. It's made all over the world and ranges from the bone-dry to the delightfully sweet. You'll want something sweet to battle spicy, aromatic takeaways, something dry for sushi and an epic, opulent Condrieu for your chicken nuggets. You lucky swine.

CAN'T FIND IT? TRY THIS:
Don't overthink it. Whatever you have in your fridge will do nicely.

COLOUR:
white

NOTABLE REGIONS:
Rhône Valley, Austria, Australia, South America

ON THE LABEL:
New World countries will always display 'Viognier' on the label. Wines from the Rhône Valley, such as Condrieu, will only state the appellation

YOU'VE JUST MOVED HOUSE

Uprooting your life every few months is sadly an inevitability in big cities, depending on whether or not your morally bankrupt landlord fancies kicking you out to convert your studio flat into a three-bed. Moving house, therefore, is less moving-van-hired-by-attractive-husband-in-a-plaid-shirt, and more frantically-summoning-two-friends-who-will-help-me-pack-my-entire-life-into-an-Uber-XL-in-under-two-minutes.

However you get from A to B, it's a bewildering joy to pull it off: the boxes are unpacked and flattened into a cardboard lasagne for the bin men, the cat is rubbing itself on the furniture, and now is the perfect time to introduce yourself to the locals. No, I don't mean knocking on the door of your *actual* neighbour. I live in London – the best I can hope for is a lukewarm half nod from a casual agoraphobe.

No, it's time to make a beeline to your local bottle shop and get to know their selection. The supermarket, post office and GP can wait. Right now, you don't need even more life admin, you need the delight of discovering a new neighbourhood through its small businesses. You need something that's been chilled in their fridges for a while, ready to uncork at a moment's notice. You need wine.

PÉT-NAT

For me, pét-nat provides an elegant solution –
there's likely a bottle to be found in your new
local. Also known as the ancestral method,
wine made in the pét-nat style is a sparkling
wine that only undergoes one fermentation,
whereas a traditional method sparkling has
two. While the wine is still fermenting and
producing CO_2, the wine is sealed with a
crown cap, which is what produces the wine's
natural effervescence. A pét-nat wine can be
made using any grape variety (although there's
a tendency to go for fruit-forward varieties).
There's something so enticingly rough and
ready about pét-nat. Pop it for ten minutes in
the fridge and sabrage it with a butter knife in
your new digs – just remember to turn the
fridge on first.

CAN'T FIND IT? TRY THIS:

This is a chance to get to know your local wine
merchant or retailer. Spend a while with them
getting to know their selection and they'll
point you in the right direction.

—

COLOUR:
anything

NOTABLE
REGIONS:
anywhere

ON THE LABEL:
you don't even need
to look at the label
for this one, if it's
sealed with a crown
cap (like a beer)
you'll know it's a
pét-nat

EUROVISION PARTY

It's not an exaggeration when I say that Eurovision is the highlight of my year. With the dedication, research and pre-game that most bring to their wedding day, I bestow upon one choice night in May.

Eurovision is more than deserving of public holiday status. It combines the childlike joy of Christmas with the sex appeal of Halloween; the whimsy of Easter with the hangover of the August Bank Holiday.

If you're just as dedicated to the study and comprehension of Eurovision lore as I, then you'll no doubt be throwing a party. Among my friendship group, it's an eclectic celebration of all the ways to get drunk around the world: German beer, Russian vodka, but the centrepiece, undoubtedly, should be the wine. What other alcoholic beverage has been made so widely across the continent, and to such exciting variations?

There is, clearly, so much more on offer than the cursory suggestion I offer below. The heritage of European winemaking is unequalled, comprising countless indigenous varieties, ancient techniques and iconic producers. It's very remiss to only suggest one European wine to try. It's like only recommending one restaurant, or one sex position – it's always nice to get a tip, but it would be a little odd to end your journey there. This is why, as well as my choice below, you'll also find a lengthy list of wines that span the continent, each worthy of a perfect *douze points*.

GRÜNER VELTLINER

Often shortened to Grüner by annoying people such as myself, Grüner Veltliner is a favourite of much of central Europe – what better way to toast to Eurovision? It's the most widely planted grape in Austria, known for its aromatic, savoury quality, with a peppery, spicy top note. The finest examples are oak-aged and can be exceptionally long-lived, but the style I want to be guzzling as I look on, bemused, at Australia, is a youthful, spicy style made in an inert vessel such as stainless steel.

COLOUR:
white

NOTABLE REGIONS:
Austria, Czech Republic, Slovakia, Hungary

ON THE LABEL:
it will nearly always say 'Grüner Veltliner' on the label

CAN'T FIND IT? TRY THIS:

Here are some fun European wines that will ensure your evening is just as diverse in liquids as it is in language. Try peachy Alsatian Gewürztraminer (white), deep Austrian Zweigelt (red), spritzy Spanish Txakoli (white), flavourful Portuguese red blends, aromatic German Riesling (white), vin gris Ploussard from the Jura, Bläufrankisch from the Czech Republic (red) and Assyrtiko from Greece (white). Get a big group together and challenge everyone to get a bottle each.

HOLIDAY

YOU'RE ON A PLANE

Maybe it's the fact that I'm financially doomed to fly economy for the rest of my life, but planes are never as glamorous as they're made out to be. I didn't go on a plane until I was 16: I had visions of being greeted by the lullaby league and gently guided into my seat, where I could drink all the Champagne and eat all the Pringles I liked. Did flying live up to my expectations? The short answer is no. The longer, angrier answer involves a dense rant about nuked food wrapped in plastic, dry, flaky skin, early-onset varicose veins and *Marley & Me*.

Thus, I make it my own, self-imposed mission to get slightly drunk on every single flight I'm ever on. No one told me to make up this rule, upon which I've imposed a strictness that no one else upholds except me. All I know is the quicker I have a couple of drinks and a little nap, the sooner I'll arrive at my destination. The 5pm hangover is future Hannah's problem.

Wine is always available on a plane, but it's rarely any good. It's also well worth noting that scientists have found that low air pressure affects our taste buds, lowering our perception of saltiness and sweetness. This is why all airplane food tastes like if Bella Italia made prison food. So, what does this mean for wine? Well, it means that you're going to need something bold to bolster the remaining taste buds you have at 35,000 feet. You'll also likely be picking from a short list of simple wines. Unless you're flying Emirates. In which case, enjoy your Krug.

MALBEC

I've been on a few budget airlines this year, and nearly all of them had a Malbec on board. This, for me, is a brilliant option. It's a wine I'm sure many of you will be familiar with. It's Argentina's most widely planted grape but originated from southwest France. It's full-bodied, high alcohol, with notes of plum, berries, vanilla and tobacco.

CAN'T FIND IT? TRY THIS:

You'll probably need something red as most simple white wines are going to be far too delicate and aromatic to get picked up by your defunct taste buds. Keep an eye out for Merlot, Tempranillo or Cabernet Sauvignon on your inflight menu.

—

COLOUR:
red

NOTABLE
REGIONS:
France, Argentina, Bordeaux

ON THE LABEL:
100% Malbec wines will nearly always say 'Malbec' on the label

YOU'RE ON A BOAT

Suffix the words 'on a boat' to a simple sentence, and life becomes that bit more glamorous. I'm reading a magazine . . . on a boat. I'm leaving you and taking the kids . . . on a boat. I'm drinking alone . . . on a boat. Yes, even acts you wouldn't be caught dead doing (but definitely do anyway, weekly), seem lavish, even debonair, reclining on a boat.

Unless we're counting ferries from Dover, I've only been on a *proper* boat once. The first and only time I went to Sorrento, I got a small boat from Sorrento to Capri. The boat was so small, however, that it was impossible to be left alone by the other groups taking the same journey, much to my distress. It was a Booking.com *White Lotus*. The Magnolia Lotus.

The only thing that quelled my growing anxiety levels caused by strangers talking to me was the wine on offer. Prosecco to kick things off, naturally, but then a delicious, crisp white to lubricate the rest of the journey to Capri. I can't remember the exact wine, but it was so unbelievably fitting for the moment. Whether you're on a boat, a yacht, a canal boat or a dinghy, this wine is sure to hit the spot. Saline, bracing, and as the effects of the second glass began to take effect, I started to enjoy myself. No! I didn't know that the national animal of my own country was a unicorn. Sure, we'd love to pay you a visit when we're back in the UK.

ALBARIÑO

When I'm thinking of a wine that could fit this moment, Albariño is the first thing that springs to mind. Also known as Alvarinho, Albariño is grown in Spain and Portugal, but critically in its coastal regions. It's citrusy (more lime than lemon) and salty, with a mouth-puckering acidity. Because of its proximity to the ocean, it also naturally pairs well with whatever you can pull out of the nearby sea.

CAN'T FIND IT? TRY THIS:

Wherever you are, boat or no boat, coastal white wines are a one-way ticket to feeling like you're there. Picpoul de Pinet, Vinho Verde, Muscadet, Greco di Tufo, Assyrtiko, Txakoli. The list is endless and delicious.

—

COLOUR:
white

NOTABLE REGIONS:
Portugal, Spain

ON THE LABEL:
it will nearly always say 'Albariño' on the label. It may also be a part of blends, such as Rías Baixas DO. These blends will not state that they contain Albariño

VALENTINE'S DAY

If love was ever blind, it's had laser eye surgery in recent years. I recall my dating experiences as a succession of rendezvous in spectacularly mid cocktail bars, where each date seemed unusually preoccupied with the size of my forehead, my weight or how many people I'd slept with. It's easy to feel cynical in a dating scene that's never felt more rigorous, but if you've made it this far, friend, then you need a bottle to celebrate.

Yes, if you've turned to this page, congratulations. It's safe to assume that you've become so irreversibly involved in each other's lives that participating in Valentine's Day is a nice-to-have, rather than a make-or-break. A first Valentine's Day is wrought with gift anxiety, lengthy love notes and expensive bottles of wine. All Valentine's Days thereafter are executed with some degree of irony. Although teddy bears clutching faux-satin hearts and novelty underwear will conjure a giggle, these semi-thoughtful gestures are all ultimately destined for the pedal bin.

Why not spend the money on a bottle of wine? This is surely something you're bound to *actually* use. However, there's no need to go completely nuts with trying to source the finest wines available to humanity (unless money is no object). I'm sure your beloved would appreciate something upper end that offers incredible value for money over a flashy label that's all mouth and no trousers. Don't blow the money you're meant to be saving for a deposit on a magnum of Provence rosé, lest you become another cringey statistic on why millennials don't own houses. Put down the avocado toast and the flat white and buy this instead.

AMARONE DELLA VALPOLICELLA —

Valpolicella is a region in Verona, in the northeast of Italy, with the wines predominantly made from the local Corvina grape. The simplest Valpolicella Classicos are bright and fruity like a Beaujolais, but the plushest, most indulgent styles are to be found in the Ripasso, Amarone and Recioto styles. Amarone della Valpolicella is made using grapes dried out for around three to four months in special drying houses, concentrating the sugars. Each of these wines takes a serious amount of time and effort, just like the best relationships.

COLOUR:
red

NOTABLE GRAPES:
Corvina Veronese, Rondinella and Molinara

ON THE LABEL:
it will always say 'Amarone della Valpolicella' on the label

CAN'T FIND IT? TRY THIS:
If your tastes are a little more plush, Recioto della Valpolicella is a sweeter red wine made in the same way as Amarone, with fermentation stopped early to preserve sugar. Or, if you want something a little more subdued, Valpolicella Ripasso is made by adding grape skins from Amarone production to the Classico, adding body and texture.

YOU'RE ON YOUR SUMMER HOLIDAYS

Just like an overly edited dating profile, the summer holiday offers the opportunity to discover the 'best' version of ourselves. 'Holiday you' poses coquettishly on a striped towel with an impossible thread count. 'Real you' spends days rotting in front of a laptop with a collection of half-finished coffees for company. Holiday you spends hours poring over restaurant listicles to craft a complete culinary itinerary. Real you is content with a tin of spaghetti hoops on the sofa, sometimes warm. Holiday you is always photo-ready, with long, hotdog legs that slither down to the corners of a x0.5 lens. Real you is vertically challenged.

Before real you has to deal with the negative bank balance and the hungover 8am flight back home, it's only right that holiday you should be drinking the good shit. I'm the same. On holiday, I get it in my head that I'm little orphan Annie, who lives modestly all year long and deserves an inexhaustible list of treats, most of which are bottles of wine (when in reality, I never really deny myself anything I want).

So, under the guise of treating yourself, try something that's local (I have a few suggestions for you, depending on where you find yourself), and something refreshing. Naturally, what grows together goes together, so if visiting a wine region, one should always drink the wines from the local area alongside your food.

For the sake of brevity, and to save you the embarrassment of panic-ordering Pinot Grigio no matter where you are in the world, I'm only including classic European holiday destinations near to where I live, in the UK, where you can get there for less than £50 and the wine is cheap, but too delicious to leave the borders. Obviously, there are countless wines to discover in each of the winemaking countries I name, far too many to go into depth in this short book, so consider these suggestions a starting point.

— FRANCE

No one loves French wine like the French, and who can blame them? Whether I'm on holiday on the beach or in the city, visiting France offers up the opportunity to drink the wines that are too brilliant to cross the border. The French also drink very seasonally: it's red wine from autumn onwards, moving into whites and rosés for summer. By virtue of the variety of wine the country produces, the French have access to a wonderful range of wines.

SANCERRE

Nothing screams French summer like a glass
of Sancerre, taken fresh from the ice bucket.
Sancerre is a regional wine from the Loire
made from 100% Sauvignon Blanc, but this
isn't your typical supermarket Sauvy B. The
region's chalky soils influence a textured, clean
wine, with notes of flint, citrus and stone
fruits. It's certainly not an intense wine, so it's
just as easily enjoyed on its own as it is with
fresh, seasonal French food. C'est bon.

—

COLOUR:
mainly white, with
some red and rosé

NOTABLE
GRAPES:
Sauvignon Blanc,
Pinot Noir

ON THE LABEL:
it will always say
'Sancerre' on the
label

CAN'T FIND IT? TRY THIS:
Other French Sauvignons you're likely to find
include Pouilly-Fumé, Touraine, Reuilly and
Menetou-Salon. If rosé is more your style, then
you'll probably find a great selection of
Provence rosé. For a light red that won't feel
heavy alongside a plate of charcuterie, opt for
a chilled Beaujolais, Pinot Noir or Cabernet
Franc.

— ITALY

I write this fresh off a trip to Italy, where I wanted to see first-hand what the locals were quaffing. And now, with a t-shirt tan that resembles Neapolitan ice cream, I'm armed with that info. As with many other European countries, wine in Italy is not reserved solely for special occasions. Wine is as commonplace as food.

Not only is wine produced in every region of Italy, but Italians themselves will tend to drink regionally for the food that's produced. Think Lambrusco and the cured meats of Emilia-Romagna, Super Tuscans and wild boar. Italy is one of my favourite winemaking countries, capable of producing an incredible range of wines: from once-in-a-lifetime glasses to pitch-perfect bottles for dinner. I'm going to provide a suggestion for the latter, but I really would encourage you to discover as many Italian wines as possible. Book your next visit as soon as you touch l'asfalto.

GRECO

The Greco grape isn't so commonplace in the UK, but it was on every wine menu I saw whilst I was in Italy. Campania – its homeland – is where Greco truly shines. Sulphur-rich volcanic soils are believed to impart a tension and minerality to the wines. It's aromatic and crisp, with a creamy, mouth-coating texture. Wine critic Jancis Robinson likens it to Viognier.

CAN'T FIND IT? TRY THIS:

A red wine favoured in Campania and much of southern Italy is Aglianico: a big, tannic wine that'll be a great accompaniment to the strong meat dishes of the region. If you're more of a rosé fan, check out the local rosato, which will often be made from a blend of red and white grapes that are typical of the region. This is a great way of gleaning a snapshot of a region's viticulture.

—

COLOUR:
white

NOTABLE REGIONS:
Apulia, Campania, Calabria

ON THE LABEL:
'Greco' is sometimes stated on bottles, but is often also a part of Campanian, Apulian and Calabrian blends

— SPAIN

My friends assume that, as a wine professional, I'm not looking for an easy ride in restaurants. I want a wine list as long as a Tolstoy novel, a sommelier who speaks in Klingon and an option to ask the audience. They assume wrongly. I love simplicity, especially on holiday. Put it on my table and tell me it's good. This is why I love Spain. Unless you've made a point of going to somewhere fancy, your average tapas bar is going to have a shorter wine list than you'd expect from the third-largest wine-producing country in the world. But herein lies the disarming simplicity of the Spanish wine scene. So, grab yourself a glass of the local tinto, blanco or rosado and rest assured it'll be delicious. But, if you want to discover something a bit different, read on.

TXAKOLI

Hailing from Spain's green north, white Txakoli is a wine I can't just reserve for the scarce occasions I'm in the Basque Country. As a copywriter, anything that professes to be 'perfect' for any situation makes my eyeballs roll back so far they dislocate. But with such a high acidity (making it a good match for pintxos), low ABV and slight spritz, I'm totally prepared to eat my own words, washed down with a bottle of Txakoli. Plus, the UK seems to be turning onto this perfection, so it's readily available from many IRL and URL bottle shops.

—

COLOUR:
white, with some red and rosé

NOTABLE REGIONS:
Basque Country

ON THE LABEL:
it will always say 'Txakoli' on the label

CAN'T FIND IT? TRY THIS:
For a similarly bright white, try Albariño, which is mostly produced in the Rías Baixas region, but readily available across Spain. You'll also find a lot of Spanish people drinking sherry, but there are far more examples available than the sweet, sticky stuff enjoyed by your grandmother. Seek out Manzanilla and Fino sherry for something dry, nutty and gut-bustingly refreshing.

— GREECE

Depending on what kind of holidayer you were as a teenager, Greece either smacks of Absolut Raspberry or ancient dust. Rammed all-inclusives or long historic tours in the midday sun. I'm a bit of both, but the most important thing will always be the wine, underrated as it is in the UK. Don't be so quick to disregard the unfamiliar grape varieties and wine regions. Let us not forget that the Greeks are some of the world's most ancient winemakers, and countries such as Italy and France owe their winemaking history to the Greeks who first planted vines there. Greek wines themselves, however, have only become 'a thing' in the UK in the past decade. Let your holiday serve as a blissful first introduction.

ASSYRTIKO

Indigenous to the island of Santorini, Assyrtiko is a white wine known for its incredible texture and acidity (think of it like a Greek Albariño or Sauvignon Blanc). Very mineral and very saline, this is a fabulous example of just how much a seaside vineyard location can affect a wine. It'll be available across Greece, no matter what regional food you're eating. The UK wine drinker is beginning to notice this versatility, so you can now find it in most of the big supermarkets, and certainly many speciality stores.

CAN'T FIND IT? TRY THIS:
Another Greek white worth trying is the aromatic Moschofilero grape, with more peachy notes of nectarine and nuts. Brilliantly dry and great when aged. Red wine lovers will get a lot out of Xinomavro, Greek's most popular export. Imagine if Pinot Noir and Nebbiolo had a baby: that's Xinomavro.

—

COLOUR:
white

NOTABLE REGIONS:
Santorini

ON THE LABEL:
it will nearly always say 'Assyrtiko' on the label

— PORTUGAL

I type this from my gate at Porto airport, the flex of tightly knit tannins still resting on my tongue. Pretty soon I'll wash it down with a €6 bottle of Coke Zero, but Portugal's intensely underrated wine scene is still etched in my brain. It was my first time visiting the country, and to say it exceeded my expectations would imply it in any way resembled them. I've spent time in arid, rustic areas of Alentejo, where the rosemary is roasted under the sun. I also visited Dão when its wooded, green vineyards were thick with the heat of early summer, but all the winemakers I met were united in their love for one specific Portuguese grape.

TOURIGA NACIONAL

The UK is beginning to cotton on to the brilliance of Touriga Nacional, a grape native to Portugal. It's a red grape that's one of the key components to port, but blends and varietal expressions are becoming increasingly popular. Its thick skin makes deep, inky wines with notes of blue and purple fruit, with a herbal, minty edge. If you love Cabernet Sauvignon, you'll get a lot out of Touriga Nacional.

CAN'T FIND IT? TRY THIS:

Seek out other red wines like berry-laden Alfrocheiro, Tinta Roriz (Portugal's name for Tempranillo) and juicy, delicate Baga. My favourite white wine to find on a list is an Antão Vaz blend, which tends be layered and tropical. And, of course, the spritz of Vinho Verde is always a good idea, especially if you're going out later (see page 92).

—

COLOUR:
red

NOTABLE REGIONS:
Douro, Dão

ON THE LABEL:
unless it's a varietal wine, Touriga Nacional may not be named on the label, and will be a part of a red wine blend

— GERMANY

I bloody love a cold holiday. As briefly explored in the intro to this section, there's all sorts of expectation tied into a sunny excursion. I find there's no such pressure with cold holidays. I love a trip to Germany in the winter, with no need to buy a skimpy wardrobe and, if anything, a requirement to wear even more black than I already do. German wine is characterised by varietal expressions of classic Germanic varieties, but a burgeoning modern wine scene is experimenting with foreign varieties, too.

RIESLING

German winemaking is synonymous with Riesling. The first recorded reference to Riesling dates back to 1435 and in the 90s, the variety saw a renaissance. Today, it's known as the monarch of German wine, and ranges from the bone-dry to the lusciously sticky-sweet. The driest wines (and the wines you're most likely to find by the glass) will be labelled Kabinett. Notes of green apple, flowers, beeswax and stone fruit are plentiful here.

CAN'T FIND IT? TRY THIS:

While I can't imagine any eventuality that you wouldn't be able to find a good Riesling by the glass in a German bar, allow me to offer some alternatives. German reds are getting a lot of love at the moment: seek out German Pinot Noir (also referred to as Spätburgunder) and Dornfelder. For other classic German whites, try Müller-Thurgau, Silvaner and Weißburgunder.

—

COLOUR:
white

NOTABLE REGIONS:
Mosel, Rheingau, Hungary, Austria, New Zealand, United States, Canada

ON THE LABEL:
the word 'Riesling' is unlikely to feature on a German bottle. Instead, keep an eye out for the elongated bottle shape and the different Riesling sweetness designations: Kabinett, Spätlese, Auslese, Beerenauslese, Trockenbeerenauslese and Eiswein

CAMPING

For this book, I have endeavoured, empath-like, to put myself in the shoes of many people, to tactfully imagine myself in situations I am often not, to understand how best to suggest a bottle. But, for camping, I'm struggling. If you're anything like me, you're of the firm belief that one of the reasons that we evolved to living in houses as a society was to avoid things like camping.

Just like many families in the UK, we didn't go abroad growing up, so the yearly holiday for the Crosbies was always camping. You'd think I look back on those instances of five people being squished inside a three-bedroom tent with a hazy, rose-tinted fondness, but camping was not, and never will be, for me.

So, with this in mind, let me try my hardest to understand what camping folk would want from a wine. It would have to be a wine that works just as well in unreasonable heat as it does in teeth-chattering cold. It must be something to sip when enjoying a striking view. And, if necessary, be easy to make mulled, should the temperature dictate the need for something a little more warming.

SHIRAZ

I used to hate Shiraz (or Syrah, as it's called in France), but I realised I wasn't drinking the right stuff. Overly oaked Shiraz contains overpowering notes of vanilla (if that's your thing, go ham), whereas classic examples have magically warming, perfumed notes of peppercorn, plum and dark berries. It's since become one of my favourites. If it's going to be chilly, pop it in your flask to keep it at room temperature, or heat it up with some spices for a boozy alternative to a cuppa.

CAN'T FIND IT? TRY THIS:
If you can't find a Shiraz, go for a French Syrah. It's the same grape but treated in an altogether different manner. Most Rhône blends are largely Syrah, so look for labels that say Côtes du Rhône, Côte-Rôtie, St-Joseph, Crozes-Hermitage, Hermitage or Cornas (these are the appellations you'll most likely find in-store).

—

COLOUR:
red

NOTABLE
REGIONS:
Australia, South
Africa

ON THE LABEL:
it will nearly always
say 'Shiraz' on the
label

YOU'VE BEEN
CAUGHT IN THE RAIN

There are plenty of situations in this book that could very well take place when it's raining outside, where you move your gaze from laughing with a friend or lover to looking over your shoulder at the rain falling down the window. You giggle with mirth, in the schadenfreude-laden knowledge that you're nice and cosy inside, while there is someone outside getting wet.

It's not so fun when the kitten heel is on the other foot, and you're transformed from the vision of metropolitan allure to a skidding and sniffling sea witch, concerned only with survival and which nearby shops have awnings.

The downpour may have caught you on your way somewhere which compels the purchase of a bottle of wine anyway, but now things are different, a new set of needs have taken precedent. What once seemed like a crisp, invigorating bottle of Pinot Grigio now appears as needlessly chilly and a one-way ticket to Flu-ville. Duck into your nearest Tesco Express or Sainsbury's and find something warming for the day ahead. A bottle of red that's bountiful in tannin, alcohol and plummy fruit – that's my advice for getting caught in the rain.

If you were waiting on a nauseating joke about piña coladas, go and reply to that mixologist on Hinge to get your fix.

PORTUGUESE RED BLEND

As the star of Portuguese wine (that isn't port) rises, it's becoming readily available in any supermarket that you might duck into from the rain, big or small. Because Portuguese wine blossomed in its own bubble, there are over 350 distinctive indigenous grape varieties to discover, and many of them are swirled into the country's sumptuous red blends. There are many to explore (I've listed some key regions to look out for, see right) but they tend to be warming, tannic and concentrated wines that will warm you from the inside out.

CAN'T FIND IT? TRY THIS:

Other warming wines for damp days include: Tempranillo (the grape used to make Rioja), Merlot, Bordeaux blends (more info on these on page 177), Grenache, Zinfandel/Primitivo and Rhône reds. Basically, anything you can grab that has warming, supple tannins and a sumptuous generosity of fruit.

—

COLOUR:
red

NOTABLE GRAPES:
Tinta Roriz, Castelão, Touriga Nacional and dozens of others

ON THE LABEL:
keep an eye out for the names of regions such as Douro, Alentejo, Lisboa, Dão, Tejo, Beira and Bairrada on the label. Look out for wines labelled 'Tinto' (meaning red)

YOU'RE IN THE SNOW

This year, I went to a skiing resort for the first time but didn't go skiing. Never learnt. Came for the views, stayed for the carbs. Spent a lot of time drinking. My aprés was also an avant and pendant. This earned me a lot of weird looks from the plankers. Rich people will look straight into your eye and ask you if you ski, as if it's some strange birthright, as if they emerged from their mother's womb on skis, slaloming between her legs, glass of Whispering Angel in hand.

At 10,000 feet, I was the coldest I'd ever been. Naturally, this means that most red wines are out of the question. It's for the same reason that you wouldn't chill most red wines. Too cold, and the subtle fruit notes will get smothered, making the tannins and alcohol appear more astringent and burning.

Also, if you're doing a snow activity that requires you to be several thousand feet above sea level, as discussed in the section of this book concerning drinking on planes (see page 146), a higher altitude will dull the palate and perception of flavour. So, what to drink?

CAVA

I think a sparkling wine like a simple Cava is a great shout. Cava is a Spanish sparkling wine (arguably *the* Spanish sparkling wine) made in the same Méthode Traditionnelle as

—

COLOUR:
white or rosé
(sparkling)

NOTABLE
GRAPES:
Macabeo, Parellada,
Xarel·lo are the most
popular grapes used

ON THE LABEL:
it will always say
'Cava' on the label

Champagne. It's light, acidic and best served cold, so you'll have no problems getting some balanced refreshment out of your glass.

CAN'T FIND IT? TRY THIS:
There's a reason you see all of the richest people you know drinking rosé on their winter holidays. A steely, mineral rosé is going to be brilliant chilled. Opt for something from Provence or the Languedoc. Failing that, some Spanish rosés taste brilliant when cold too. Despite what I said above, don't completely discount red wines: a simple, fruity wine like a Beaujolais will taste delicious chilled. When it comes to sparkling wines, the simpler and zestier the better, so no need to crack open the vintage Champagne.

BONFIRE NIGHT

Bonfire Night. The British Burning Man festival. We make an effigy, make a massive fire, burn said effigy, toast marshmallows on its embers and then get so cold we go home. It'd be nicer if it was held on a hazy summer evening, with sand between our toes, Coachella style. But alas, it's held on 5th November, the very day Guy Fawkes' plan to go full demolition crew on the Houses of Parliament was foiled.

Wine doesn't just need to be a lubricant for the squeaky wheel that is social interaction. It needs to help you survive the cold too (why is it always raining on Bonfire Night?). There is new research that suggests wine actually does make you warmer. So, at such a time that you're freezing your ass off, a bottle can help get the blood flowing. Alcohol is something called a vasodilator, which means that it increases blood flow in the vessels nearest to the skin (hence why some people get a flush when they drink). It also affects the part of the brain that senses temperature, meaning the proverbial wine jacket is very much . . . verbial?

CHIANTI

It simply must be a full-bodied red – something that sings when sipped by the fire. Let's go for Chianti. Mmmmm, Chianti. Warming, herbaceous, spicy Chianti. From central Tuscany, this blend is Sangiovese-dominant, meaning it's savoury and spicy, with each heady mouthful going straight to your belly. If it says 'Chianti Classico', that means it's from the historic centre of the region.

CAN'T FIND IT? TRY THIS:

Similarly tannic, high-alcohol wines include Bordeaux, Cabernet Sauvignon, Syrah and Tempranillo. The list goes on. Just seek out something that's above 13% and you'll be toasty.

—

COLOUR:
red

NOTABLE GRAPES:
75–100% Sangiovese, up to 10% Canaiolo and up to 20% of any other permitted varieties

ON THE LABEL:
it will always say 'Chianti' on the label

CHRISTMAS

Welcome to the festive section of the book. But this is not a Christmas wine guide as you know it. Firstly, I'm not going to waste your time recommending wines that can only be bought in a speciality wine shop in Beaune, because I know you're currently reading this section gazing in horror at the barren shelves of a Tesco Express. Secondly, I am categorically not going to talk about pairing wine with turkey. I thought I made it clear that this was not a wine pairing book (didn't you read the introduction?). I'm not the type to submit myself to the festive masochism that is consuming mouthful after mouthful of arid turkey. At Christmas, we drink wine to celebrate, not lubricate. If you want to know what to pair with turkey, look elsewhere.

Instead, I want to write about wines that will match the moment. The *real* moment. For many – even for those who don't celebrate it as a religious holiday – Christmas is about togetherness and excess, enjoyed over any food you bloody well like. With this in mind, I'm going to make three suggestions on a sparkling, red and white that I feel will contribute to the warm fuzzies, with consideration given to the fact that your family may only live near a poorly stocked supermarket.

THE SPARKLING: CRÉMANT DE LOIRE

Crémant de Loire uses the same labour-intensive Méthode Traditionnelle as Champagne. The best examples show similar notes of exuberant green fruits, balanced by a brioche depth. But Hannah, I hear you cry, why not just get Champagne, then? Because you'll be able to secure three bottles of Crémant de Loire for the price of one Grande Marque Champagne and I *know* you're not about to traipse around the shop (with possible children/dog/partner in tow), queue for the lifetime of a small mammal and cut off all circulation to your fingers taking the bags to the car just for *one* bottle of fizz. After all that drama, it'll be the first thing on your mind when you get home. I know you want, nay, *require*, at least three bottles of the stuff: one as a pat on the back for doing the shop itself, one on Christmas Day and one on Boxing Day. Plus, if it's a last-minute affair, a Crémant is more likely to have been left on the shelf by the Christmas hordes.

COLOUR:
white (sparkling)

NOTABLE REGIONS:
Anjou-Saumur, Touraine

NOTABLE GRAPES:
mostly Chenin Blanc, but can also contain Chardonnay, Cabernet Franc, Cabernet Sauvignon and Pineau d'Aunis

ON THE LABEL:
it will nearly always say 'Crémant de Loire' on the label

CAN'T FIND IT? TRY THIS:
Crémant de Bourgogne, Crémant de Bordeaux, Crémant d'Alsace, Crémant de Limoux or Méthode Cap Classique from South Africa are all other examples made using the Méthode Traditionnelle.

THE WHITE: MÂCON-VILLAGES

White wines don't feature nearly as heavily as sparkling or reds at the average Christmas, so let's not go too crazy. For a Christmas white: something that'll be readily stocked nearby, but a couple notches above your bog-standard corner shop Pinot Grigio. I think a wine from the Mâconnais will hit the spot. This is Burgundy's most southerly area, known to wine insiders as a place to go to find *really* good value Burgundy that you don't need to sell your dog to buy. It's 100% Chardonnay but the Mâconnais' warmer climate yields a ripe, inviting wine. Most supermarkets tend to have their own-label Mâcon-Villages.

—

COLOUR:
white

NOTABLE GRAPES:
Chardonnay

ON THE LABEL:
it will always say 'Mâcon-Villages' on the label

CAN'T FIND IT? TRY THIS:
Any Chardonnay, your local will have at least one, whether it's from the New or Old World. You might have heard of Pouilly-Fuissé, a famous wine from the same Mâconnais region, try that for something a little more full-bodied.

THE RED: RED BORDEAUX (CLARET)

Don't come for me. I know I just said that this 'wasn't going to be your normal festive wine guide' about two minutes ago, but some classics are classics for good reason. Red Bordeaux (or Claret, as it's also called) is well-known enough that it'll be readily available in the run up to Christmas, and some offer extraordinarily good value, especially the own-branded bottles from specialist shops. Keep an eye out for places like Saint-Émilion, Saint-Julien or Haut-Médoc on the label: those are appellations of reliable quality that may be stocked in a supermarket. However, all examples of red Bordeaux will happily complement an array of hearty Christmas dishes, each with a deep, satisfying finishing that goes all the way to your belly. Happy belly = merry Christmas.

CAN'T FIND IT? TRY THIS:
Varietal examples of Bordeaux's constituent parts – Cabernet Sauvignon, Cabernet Franc or Merlot – would be a good alternative here.

—

COLOUR:
red

NOTABLE GRAPES:
predominantly a blend of Cabernet Sauvignon, Merlot and Cabernet Franc, with small amounts of Petit Verdot and Malbec permitted

ON THE LABEL:
unless the bottle is marked 'Bordeaux Supérieur', it's unlikely you'll see the word 'Bordeaux' on the label. Instead, keep an eye out for names of châteaux and appellations (head to page 25 to see if the name on the bottle is an appellation)

BOXING DAY / BETWIXTMAS

What can I say about Boxing Day that hasn't already been wryly dissected by countless other writers? Boxing Day marks the start of a period of time recently coined 'Betwixtmas', where everything sort of melds into one. What day is it? When was the last time I washed my hair? Am I eating Ferrero Rocher or foil? Do I really care?

Gatsby-like revelry has subsided and, in its place, a much more gentle sense of celebration. Most of us are still not back at work for a few days, so there's no sense in taking down the decorations just yet. Holiday rules still apply, which, obviously, means alcohol consumption is permitted at all hours.

The special-occasion wines have all been opened on Christmas Day, the Champagne has been toasted, and you've been left feeling a little delicate (if you're feeling especially sorry for yourself, turn to page 132). I talk about drinking wines and thinking wines a lot, but you definitely need a drinking wine in this instance – a wine that is made for uninterrupted quaffing as opposed to lengthy, meaningful discussion. You require something that'll keep the festivities going but will be gentler on the palate and will pair effortlessly with the cold cuts as you watch *Morecambe and Wise* in your pants. Normal service will resume soon.

CHINON

My go-to if I'm looking for easy, thirst-quenching drinking that goes with a variety of fares. Found in the Loire Valley, Chinon can indeed be tannic and spicy, but the style of Chinon that I want when the party's over is the joyous, blackberry-scented tipple that's served in the wine bars of Paris. The spice is still there, yes, but it's a sprinkle of festive star anise, rather than the whole bloody rack. So juicy, you barely care it's yet another bottle of wine to take to the bins tomorrow.

CAN'T FIND IT? TRY THIS:
Other Loire Cab Francs include Saumur-Champigny, Bourgueil and Touraine, but again, make sure you find the lighter examples, unless you have a particular aversion to sobriety during Christmastime.

—

COLOUR:
mostly red, with a small amount of white and rosé

NOTABLE GRAPES:
Cabernet Franc; up to 25% Cabernet Sauvignon is permitted

ON THE LABEL:
it will always say 'Chinon' on the label

NEW YEAR'S EVE

On the last 31st December, I spent over half an hour in my local bottle shop, poring over their wine choices for the evening ahead. I don't like anyone to take too long to do anything. I'm the person who passive-aggressively sighs with all the impatience of Veruca Salt when someone halts the pedestrian flow. I'm embarrassingly quick to snap when trying to show my parents how to accept something on AirDrop. And yet there I was, standing in front of the wine racks, with something less than a clue.

Thing is, I usually know exactly what I want to grab for New Year's Eve, and I'm out before the lovely shop assistant can even begin to form the words 'carbonic maceration' in their brain. But this was the first NYE I would be consciously spending at home, with no shapewear and no videos of me dishing out dance moves that resemble me being tazed violently.

What do you drink when no one's watching? What bottle do you get if it's just you? Is it the same one you'd buy if you were opening it in a room full of your friends? I know exactly what I'd get if I was celebrating with other people. But New Year's Eve isn't about other people, it's about you. It's what *you* want to do. It's about celebrating the gift of another year in *your* life. And you can drink whatever you bloody well like.

BLANC DE NOIRS

For me, I don't think it could be anything else. Blanc de Noirs is a type of Champagne made using only the dark-skinned Pinot Noir and Pinot Meunier. Yes, it's on the spenny side and I'm by no means a 'manifesting' devotee, but there's surely something to be said for kicking off the year sipping some of the finest, most complex fizz known to man. Drink as you mean to go on. Drink for pleasure. Drink like no one's watching.

CAN'T FIND IT? TRY THIS:
There's plenty of English sparkling made using Pinot Noir and Pinot Meunier that'll conjure up those same generous layers than envelop the palate. Failing that, seek out a Méthode Cap Classique from South Africa, which will offer the richness you seek from a Blanc de Noirs.

—

COLOUR:
white (sparkling)

NOTABLE GRAPES:
Pinot Noir, Pinot Meunier

ON THE LABEL:
some Champagnes will say 'Blanc de Noirs' on the label, but some won't, even if they're 100% Pinot Noir and/or Pinot Meunier. It's best to look on the back of the bottle to see if there's a blend breakdown

NEW YEAR'S DAY

Give yourself a rest, for Christ's sake.

ACKNOWLEDGEMENTS

To begin at the beginning, I'd like to thank my incredible English teachers. In alphabetical order: Mr Cameron, Mr Keeley and Ms Terry. You were the ones who made me feel like I could write, and that it was a path I could follow. Without you, this book wouldn't exist and I'd probably be doing something.I hate.

I'd like to thank Charlie Geoghegan, Mike Daw and Sophie Wyburd, who all read early extracts of this book, stroked my fragile ego and reassured me I was on the right track. A special thanks is owed to Sophie, who got pregnant with a book baby at the same time as me. Not only are you a brilliant friend, confidante and podcast host, but your advice during the writing process has been the most invaluable to me. I can't wait to read *Tucking In*.

Thank you to the writing teams I've been a part of throughout my career in wine. I've learned something from every single one of you: Amy, Will and Molly-Sue at Majestic; Milo, Charlie (again), Issariya and Barbara at Berry Bros. & Rudd; and Stu, Su, Jo, Steve, Martin and Amy (again) at The Wine Society. How do you tie down a snarling, complex, beautiful beast like wine and possibly find the words to tame it? Thanks to you all, I'm somewhat closer to the answer.

A huge thank you is also due to my team at Hot Sauce: Siobhan, Katy, Yas and Joyce. Not only may you most be the most beautiful group of women that have ever worked in talent management, but you have also changed my life completely, for the better. Thank you for being so wonderfully patient and for organising my life. I'd also like to thank Martine from Sauce Communications, who gave me such a valuable insight when I first wrote the proposal for Corker.

At Ebury, many, many, many thanks are owed to Lara McLeod, Morgana Chess and Demeter Scanlon, but particularly to Celia Palazzo, my editor and the number one champion of this book. I knew I wanted to end up with Ebury from the second I met you all over a bottle of Chenin Blanc. Thank you for your thoughtful edits, your belief in this book and the 'LOL's in your feedback notes.

Thank you to all my friends, but particularly my Sunday sessions friendship group who let me neurotically rant to them about being a tortured, knackered writer, particularly Oliver, Renata, Angus, Becca, Frankie, and especially, especially Jake. Thank you for putting up with me.

Most of all, I'd like to thank my wonderful, incredible family for supporting me throughout my life — book notwithstanding. In ascending age order, thank you to Millie, without whom I doubt I'd have as good a sense of humour as I do. To Martha, for being a constant inspiration to not let the bastards grind me down, and for being such a fabulous, inspiring presence whichever room you walk in to. To my mum, Nicky, who remains unrivalled in being the kindest, most understanding person I've ever, ever met. Every foster child you look after is lucky to call you their social worker, and I am even luckier to call you my mum. To my dad Brian, to whom I attribute pretty much everything creative I've ever done. Thank you for being the best musician, writer, woodworker, bird-spotter, critical thinker, and for bestowing me with a pretty much perfect taste in music. Not many are lucky enough to have a family like ours, and I doubt I'd be anywhere much at all right now without your patience and love.

Thank you, thank you, thank you.

INDEX

Page numbers in **bold** indicate a main entry

ABOUT THE AUTHOR

Hannah Crosbie is a wine writer and broadcaster from Edinburgh. She poured her first bottle in a restaurant before she was legally old enough to do so, and has been fascinated by wine, food and restaurant culture ever since. She worked as a copywriter for many retailers and importers before becoming a freelance wine writer and broadcaster as a regular wine presenter on Sunday Brunch. She now writes for *The Evening Standard*, *The Independent* and Mob, with occasional bylines in *Decanter* and *Club Oenologique*. In 2020, she founded Dalston Wine Club, an inclusive event series that has seen her write and curate wine lists and programmes for Soho House and The Hoxton. She resides, eternally, in East London.